# Saving the World

# Saving the World

## THE SPIRITUALIZATION OF MATTER

### Henry Guy

VOX SOPHIA
PUBLISHING
2002

COPYRIGHT © 2002 BY HENRY GUY
All rights reserved. No part of this book may be reproduced in any form or by any means, electronic or mechanical, including photocopying, recording, or by any information storage and retrieval system, without permission in writing from the publisher, except in the case of brief quotation embodied in critical reviews and certain other uses permitted by copyright law.

VOX SOPHIA PUBLISHING
5900 Klinger
Arlington, Texas 76016
817-429-8299    Fax: 817-429-2429
Sales only: 877-245-6813 (toll-free)
www.voxsophia.org    sales@voxsophia.org

ORDERING INFORMATION
Special discounts are available on quantity purchases. Please contact the publisher. An order form is on the last page of the book.

PRINTED IN THE UNITED STATES OF AMERICA
♻ Printed on acid-free, recycled paper.

PUBLISHER'S CATALOGING-IN-PUBLICATION
Guy, Henry, 1946-
    Saving the world : the spiritualization of matter /
Henry Guy. -- 1st ed.
    p. cm.
    Includes bibliographical references and index.
    LCCN: 2001088426
    ISBN: 0-9708352-0-5
    1. Spiritual life--New Age movement. 2. New Age movement.
        I. Title.

BP605.N48G89 2002            299'.93
                             QB101-201073

FIRST EDITION
06 05 04 03 02   10 9 8 7 6 5 4 3 2 1

*Dedicated*

To D. K.

for using words to teach the limitation of words
and the inspiration to go beyond them.

# Contents

| | | |
|---|---|---|
| Foreword | | ix |
| Introduction | | 1 |
| 1. | It's Who We Are | 9 |
| | Identity Is a Process | |
| | The Savior Trapped in Duality | |
| | A Perspective on Duality | |
| 2. | Redemption: Spiritualization of Matter | 21 |
| | Redeeming in the Physical World | |
| | Redeeming in the Emotional World | |
| | Redeeming in the Mental World | |
| 3. | Why It Is So Difficult | 41 |
| | The Trance of Materiality | |
| | The World We Made | |
| | The Problem of Hierarchy | |
| | Vision: Our Hope | |
| | Vision: Our Problem | |
| 4. | Unity | 61 |
| | The Problem Is the Order | |
| | The Power of Inclusion | |
| | The Individual Life and the Group Life | |

5. THE WORLD TEACHER AND RELIGIONS ... 73
   Waking Up Is Hard to Do
   Truth, Meaning, and Symbols
   The Confusion
   One Truth, Unique Meanings,
      and Diverse Symbols

6. THE ROLE OF THE KINGDOMS IN NATURE ... 93
   Kingdoms in Nature
   The Fifth Kingdom
   The First Brother
   The World Servers

7. THERE IS A PLAN ... 107
   Our Part
   The Birth of Love

8. THE NEXT STEP ... 123
   Work in the Economic Field
   Work in the Political Field
   Work in the Field of Education
   Right Human Relations

9. GREATER THINGS ... 141

RESOURCES ... 145

INDEX ... 147

# Foreword

The evolutionary process for human beings on our planet *can* be explained in such a compelling way that one finds oneself entering into it personally, deliberately choosing to strive for the next required step for oneself and for humanity as a whole.

Conditions that are carefully brought to mind in this book would move us to immediate action if we had just arrived here with our present mental faculties intact. We would observe without the prejudices that accrue from being immersed in the life of every day. We suddenly would achieve a clarity of perception about how human beings relate to one another as individuals and in groups. We would realize the interdependence that exists among all the kingdoms in nature, including the human. It would be crystal clear how simple adjustments in the attitudes and actions of human beings could bring about world-shaking changes for the better. Above all, we would be aware of the almost insurmountable illusions to which most people are subject in earth life that are keeping them from realizing those simple adjustments.

Without the aforesaid advantage of late arrival, it is useful to have a few with us such as the author, who have struggled to reach beyond the illusions and find themselves called to clue in the rest of us.

In the depths of our hearts we yearn to discover solutions to the mysteries of our present troubled existence. It is a relief to know that we are not, after all, helpless in our human plight, what seems to be unending mismanagement of our world and relationships, individually and en masse. We sense there is a responsibility to make the necessary alterations, both as individuals and as the human race. Imagined inadequacy leads us to embrace complacency.

The beautiful and completely natural way out of the melee is carefully put before us in this book.

Gloria Crook, Ph.D.
*Founding president*
*School of Ageless Wisdom*
*and Robert Muller School*

# *Acknowledgments*

While this book has but one author, it is the result of more than two decades of work with the School of Ageless Wisdom in Arlington, Texas, U.S.A. (www.unol.org/saw). At this school, a small group of students meet together several times per week for study and discussion of the Ageless Wisdom as found in the twenty-four books of esoteric philosophy by Alice Bailey. Without the insight, input, and the living example of the other students, this book would not exist.

Two members of this group have contributed greatly. Dr. Gloria Crook read all the drafts and offered wise editorial and design counsel; Dr. Crook also wrote the foreword. Leslie Vann also offered editorial suggestions and worked energetically to network for peer review.

Many of the peer reviewers offered suggestions that greatly helped the presentation. Among these reviewers are Jon Caswell, Kathy Crater, Vicki Johnston, Diane Moody, Starshine Nolan, Rene Prieto, and Lidia Shkorkina.

I would like to thank Sharon Goldinger at PeopleSpeak (www.detailsplease.com/peoplespeak) for copyediting and Cathy Hunt (www.portfolios.com/clhdesign) for a beautiful cover.

I would also like to express my heartfelt gratitude to my family, and especially to Judy, for the understanding a project like this demands.

# Introduction

To most of us, saving the world seems like a beautiful, yet distant, ideal. Generally, we don't have a crystal-clear idea of what saving the world would be, but we are certain that it would be bigger than the scale of our lives. We hope it happens, but we are sure the task will take someone more powerful and capable than ourselves. After all, we have our own lives and our own problems.

Saving the whole world may seem too overwhelming for one person, but saving part of the world does not. For most of us, the urge to save is such an integral part of ourselves that it shows itself as a reflex. If we see a child fall into a rushing river, we dive in. We don't wait and weigh the pros and cons. We don't care whether we like or dislike her. We don't worry that we may lose our own lives; we dive in to save her.

Saving is so much a part of us, we have institutionalized it. When disaster leaves some of us bleeding, dazed, hungry, or homeless, the Red Cross and the Red Crescent send aid. When famine threatens, the UN's World Food Programme and countless religious organizations send help. When political unrest chases people from their homes,

Doctors Without Borders and the UN High Commissioner for Refugees send help. If we have a life-threatening illness or accident, medical professionals help save our lives. Psychological professionals help save us from fear, depression, anger, and addiction.

The current of saving runs so deep within our lives that we could say it is the story of humanity. Of all the possible themes, saving is the basis for almost all our literature. The basic story is always the same: Some disaster or problem looms. The character cannot solve the problem by the usual means. Destruction threatens. The situation calls forth something from deep within the character, some power unknown until that time. The character, using the newly found power, solves the problem, rights the wrong, and saves the day. Good triumphs over evil and the character emerges as a hero. The saving may be grand or tiny, whole or partial, but saving is the unfailing plot to all our stories. Whether the story of the hero is about Rosa Parks, Luke Skywalker, or Jesus, we never stop repeating it.

What is this power that can lift us out of our everyday existence? Although I had a personal experience with it, the power to save remains mysterious. It happened about twenty years ago. I was swimming at a beach with my family and some friends. It was hot and sunny, and I was lying down, recovering from far too much good food. The heat and the food left me in that half-awake/half-asleep state. Before I knew what was happening, I bolted to my feet and ran out into the water. My four-year-old daughter's friend was standing in the murky water with a worried look on her face. My body was leaping through the water, yet my brain had still not caught up with what was going on. Without knowing why, I asked, "Where is she?" The little girl pointed and I dove. In a few seconds I pulled my drowning daughter from the water.

Here is what is so difficult to understand about that experience: The little friend had not called out. No one on the beach had any idea that my daughter was in trouble. I was not even partly aware of what was going on until I pulled my daughter into the air. After she was safe, a flood of realization hit me: another part of me that was not a regular visitor to my brain knew what my usual self didn't know. Over the years, there grew a deep knowing that this part of me didn't want to save just my daughter, it wants to save everybody. Saving is its nature and its purpose.

I began to recognize this "saving force" at work all through the world. Yes, it saves us from danger and disaster, but it also works through redemption and liberation. It saves us from our illusions and from institutions we've outgrown. We used to believe that the world was flat. We used to believe that slavery was a good idea. We used to believe that revenge was good. We used to believe that women were property. We used to believe that time was absolute. We used to believe that love was a weakness. We have been saved from these illusions, and our lives are fuller and richer for it.

This saving force is at work in other ways. Many of us are prisoners of our own criticism, hate, jealousy, and many other negative emotions. We can spend years trapped in the bad feelings arising from some offense committed against us. We can worry ourselves (and others) into ill health over trifles. Unreasonable fears can hold us for decades. Yet many of us find a way to free ourselves from these prisons. We learn to be less judgmental, more understanding, courageous, and forgiving. As we learn these difficult lessons, we are saving our little part of the world. We have refused to live something less by choosing something greater.

Why are we so fascinated with the story of a savior? Because it's us, the best part of us. Saving is our story and our reason for living. Behind that veneer of brain and blood lives a savior in each of us. This savior is trying its best to get our attention, engage us, and save the world. This savior can get into the lives of some of us better than others. If it extends its influence into our brains and hearts, we cannot see life the same as we did before. Human history is filled with such individuals. Our countless heroes and saviors are proof that the saving force finds its way into our lives.

In this book, I hope to do five things. For one, I hope to help us remember how basic the idea of saving is in our lives. It is true that we do not think very often of saving the world, but largely that's true because we are so busy doing it. I hope to show that saving on some level or another is what we do, and we do it because of who we are.

For another, I hope to show that the problems and obstacles that make our lives so difficult are integral to saving. In saving, we transform these obstacles from the worst part of our lives to the best. This transformation is spiritualization. Whether we consider it individually or collectively, it is the very purpose for which we are born on Earth.

I am also seeking to help in a great preparation. Whether we know it or not, we are readying ourselves to save the world, the whole world. Few of us believe this now because we hold an idea of our lives as being too small and insignificant to make a real difference in a project of that size. Our sense of proportion is correct: one person could never save the whole world. But we are on our way to becoming individuals plus something much greater. That something is who we are together. Who we are together can and will save the world.

I also hope to show that we are not alone in this grand project. Our need to save is sparked by the impelling purpose of the Creator of this sweet, lovely planet Earth. Our Creator works through groups, involving all the kingdoms in nature, both the ones evident to us and those not so evident.

Finally, I hope to show that a plan exists for saving the world and that each of us has a part to play. The seemingly overwhelming problems facing humanity are but a part of this plan. We must take a new step, and these problems are demanding that we take it.

Saving the world is a theme of many religions, philosophies, idealistic movements, economic systems, and political systems. From Martin Luther King to King Arthur, the impulse to raise our world to something greater runs old, deep, and wide throughout the story of humankind. We may disagree on the specifics of how to accomplish it, but we generally agree that saving the world is good. This near-universal agreement is an indication that the impulse to save the world originates from our Creator. It is built into us like breathing or DNA. We *have* to do it.

Please be assured that in no way will this book seek to convert you to a religion, a philosophy, or a system of thought. However, if you come from the mechanistic perspective that holds that life is but an aberrant effect of random combinations of matter, you will probably have trouble with this book. I am writing from the perspective that life is the creative, motive energy of the universe and shows itself through all that is. All that we sense and know exists because life, one grand Life, intends it to be so.

Exploring the subject of saving the world will demand that we use some concepts and word-symbols that philosophies, religions, and systems of thought have earlier used. I have used quotes from the Christian Bible because it is in common use and many people have read and studied it. I use these quotes strictly to bring light to the subject by using words familiar to many. In no way will this book ask that you accept the authority of any religious, political, scientific, or philosophical system of thought. I hope that bringing light on the subject of saving the world will reveal some of the truth from which it springs and that this truth will be its own authority.

This book attempts to speak to the subject of saving the world from the point of view of what some call the Ageless Wisdom or Core Wisdom. The Ageless Wisdom is and has been available to humanity throughout all time. It consists of a vast body of written and unwritten information relating to certain fundamental, universal laws. Political, religious, philosophic, artistic, and scientific thought have their roots in this wisdom. With a small group of twenty or so dedicated students, I have studied and attempted to apply the Ageless Wisdom for the last twenty-five years. We study primarily the twenty-four books of esoteric philosophy by Alice A. Bailey.[1] It is from persistent meditation on the concepts found in the works of Alice Bailey that much of this book came to life.

---

[1] These books are available at *www.lucistrust.org* or by contacting Lucis Publishing Company, 120 Wall Street, 24th Floor, New York, New York, 10005.

You may find that some of the concepts and word-symbols used in this book seem old. You may have heard them repeatedly presented in some school of thought, philosophy, or religion. Please try to dissociate the connotations you may carry from the simple meaning intended here. However, you may find that some of the concepts used in the book are new to you. Also, some (maybe many) of the concepts presented will be unverifiable. Please consider taking these concepts as a simple working hypothesis. By that I mean take the idea as a *possible* truth and try it out in your conscious, meditative life. If by using the hypothetical idea you can better save the world, and if in its use it rings ever more true, then consider it true, but not otherwise.

> *All necessary truth is its own evidence.*
> RALPH WALDO EMERSON

Some explanation of words that connote maleness might be in order. The oldest known root of the word "man" is the Sanskrit word "manus," which means "mind." "Human" means "mind-being." We are mind-beings and have no gender before we take incarnation into earthly, physical bodies. Out of incarnation we are related to each other and the universe in a completely loving way. A relationship founded in such intrinsic love is difficult to remember after we become separated, earthly beings. We typically use the unselfish, loving family as a metaphor for this relationship. Inadequate and apparently gender biased, "brother" is frequently used to symbolize our spiritual relationship with each other, and it is our collective spiritual identity that the word "brotherhood" so inadequately seeks to symbolize. When I use the words "brother" and "brotherhood" I am not trying to exclude or include females. I am seeking words in common usage that symbolize our relationship exclusive of gender. I will also use the word "he" to represent God in the third person, knowing that both of the terms "he" and "God" anthropomorphize, trivialize, and therefore misrepresent that awesome Truth. We need better words.

I hope that by devoting some of your valuable time and energy to this book, you can form a better and deeper understanding of saving the world and of the part in this task that you and all of us play. I also hope that by mulling over and discussing these concepts, you can draw to them your attention and perhaps your intention and thereby unleash the power that can truly save the world.

Henry Guy
Arlington, Texas
Summer 2001

# 1

# *It's Who We Are*

*Our need to save the world has its roots in our eternal identity and our eons-old purpose for existence.*

The above statement implies that we have an identity that exists throughout all time and that we are not wholly, or maybe not even slightly, conscious of it. It also implies that we have always had a purpose for existence of which we are not wholly (or even slightly) conscious. How could it be that we are eternal beings yet take ourselves to be strictly temporal? How could we spend our whole lives in the dark about our true nature? How could it be that this eternal being has a purpose for existence and we could not have the slightest notion what that purpose is?

Answering these questions is difficult partly because we don't consider them very much. Our families, schools, governments, and societies do not particularly encourage consideration of our identity and purpose for existence. Generally, we refer these deep questions to our religions. Yet most religions tread very lightly around these issues and generally do not say much about them. Many promise a change from a temporal to an eternal identity but one that happens after death. This keeps the truth of our eternal identity a mystery. As far as purpose goes, most religions enjoin us to "be good." Being good is wise and useful, but then again it does not take us very far down the road of understanding our purpose for being here.

## Identity Is a Process

It would be so easy if someone would just tell us who we really are, but identity doesn't seem to work that way. It is difficult to pin identity down. Any thoughtful, experienced individual has recognized the problem with determining his or her true identity. As soon as one defines one's identity, that definition starts to become inadequate. Identity seems to be a process. Over a lifetime, we take ourselves to be one identity and then another.

> *I still feel—kind of temporary about myself.*
> Arthur Miller

These various identities show themselves through our language. Early in life, when someone asks who we are, we repeat the name given us by our family. We naturally associate ourselves with our physical bodies: "I am little, strong, fast," and so on. Soon, we learn to identify with our emotional states: "I am happy, sad, angry," and so on. As our capabilities increase we may enlarge our identity to what we do: "I am a mother, student, consultant."

When we begin to think for ourselves, a whole new sense of identity opens up. Thinking helps us integrate all the different parts of ourselves (our bodies, feelings, and thoughts) into a sure sense of self. The mind has the ability to draw parts together into a whole, but it can also draw distinctions. It is the mind that makes it seem that we are separate from our environment and from other people. Thinking for ourselves gives us the potential to know who we are, know where we are headed, and know what is suitable and what is not. Our philosophies and religions serve only to buttress our now rock-solid worldview as individuals. Self-interest rules our lives and our relations with others. We are each an individual, a self, and we know it. Our self is of utmost importance to us. We foster it and lavish it with gifts and opportunities of every description. We see the world through the eyes of the individualized self, and that makes us self-conscious in the truest sense of the phrase.

If you have lived long enough to have had the experience of selfhood, you have probably also posed the nagging question, "But who am I, really?" We either have or will come to that question out of an urging from deep within. The success of identity as the self makes us all wonder eventually, "Is this all? Am I here purely for my own pleasure?"

> *The whole dear notion of one's own Self—marvelous old free-willed, free-enterprising, autonomous, independent, isolated island of a Self—is a myth.*
> LEWIS THOMAS

Integrated, self-oriented individuals who are tiring of the selfish life become aware of something greater than themselves. They find less and less meaning in a life lived strictly for themselves, while the "something greater" gains in importance. They look for it in religions, philosophies, the arts, sciences, philanthropy, community, or business. They can seek it out in the experiences or writings of others. Most could not tell others what it is they seek or what drives them onward in their search for a deeper meaning of existence. Most will find themselves living through periods of being on fire with deep yearning to know, followed by periods of wondering what all the fuss was about as they return to their lives of business as usual. Many find that although they may not know what is causing this dramatic change in them, they have an increasing need to reach out to and help others.

As our identity changes, our purpose for living changes. Before we know ourselves as integrated individuals, our environment and other people generally dictate our purpose for being. We don't seem to have a purpose of our own because we do not have a fully integrated person of our own. At this stage, we are interested only in meeting the necessities of survival. The integrated self, however, has a very sure purpose: make the individual life better, become more powerful, gain more influence, get richer, smarter, and more attractive.

When we tire of the self-oriented life, the purpose of our life goes from crystal-clear self-interest to a fuzzy idea of a "greater purpose." We begin to think about sharing what we have and know and to regard others as something other than rivals or people who may be of some use to us. Many individuals find themselves in this situation today. They are beginning to find out who they are *not* (a strictly self-oriented individual) but have an unclear idea of their identity now. They know that their purpose used to be self-fulfillment, but now they are not so sure what it is.

You will not find the final word on identity in these pages because there can be no final word. Life seems to be a succession of identities that carry us through a succession of states of consciousness. For most of us living subject to time and space, realizing our eternal identity and purpose for existence seems to be an ideal, a dream, or a distant vision.

Yet all of us have some thread of conscious connection to our eternal identity and purpose. Among the many possible ways, this connection shows itself through admiration. Most people admire qualities such as truthfulness, humility, sincerity, compassion, persistence, intelligence, self-sacrifice, strength, wisdom, understanding, integrity, goodwill, selflessness, creativity, inclusiveness, responsibility, as well as hundreds of others. It is no accident that we so admire these qualities. They represent both our roots and our destiny. They speak of our identity before we were born into the stuff of Earth. Our attraction to them is our promise that we are on our way to exhibiting them in fullness again.

## The Savior Trapped in Duality

The generally admired qualities, taken together, describe the savior. This ideal savior is intelligent and compassionate and an unyielding instrument of goodness in the world. The savior is pure, just, true, and self-sacrificing. We have portrayed the savior as the hero in countless stories, myths, scriptures, and biographies down through the ages. The savior rights the wrongs, heals the sick, and stands against injustice. The savior of our religions, the hero of our stories represents an ideal to which we aspire. The savior is the living truth that great goodness can live through human blood and bone. We would be the savior if we could.

When we look realistically at our own lives, it is safe to say that we do not see the ideal savior shining forth in full glory. But realistically we do see some qualities of the savior in ourselves, at least in some faint way. We do put the needs of at least some others ahead of ourselves. This is a reflection of compassion and selflessness. We persist through the difficulties of life: this is a reflection of an unyielding will. We can see what is wrong, we can tell evil from good, what should be from what is. Being able to tell this difference is the first step in saving. We may or may not stand against all odds for what is right, but at least we are smart enough to know the difference. So we do see the qualities of the savior beginning to shine through our lives. Maybe it is shining only dimly, but it shines.

In an honest look at our lives, we would find that we are also displaying qualities that we do not admire, qualities that are not heroic. Most people do not admire qualities such as arrogance, anger, pride, hatefulness, jealousy, selfishness, bigotry, evasiveness, greediness, laziness, hurtfulness, and irresponsibility, to name only a few. Most of us would also agree that these qualities are in some sense restricting or retarding our lives lived as the savior. We would love continually if we didn't lose our tempers, and we would give totally, except that we have to save some for ourselves. We would help people if they all deserved it. We all have these less admirable qualities to contend with and know that if these limitations were gone, goodness would flourish in our lives.

So who we are is an interesting mix of the savior and our own limitations. We are a blend of both qualities we admire and those we don't. This sense of duality defines most human beings. We seem to be both good and bad, saintly and profane. Paul speaks of this state of duality:

> *I know that in me (that is, in my flesh)*
> *dwells no good thing: for to will is present with me;*
> *but how to perform that which is good I find not.*
> *For the good that I would, I do not:*
> *but the evil which I would not, that I do.*
> *For I delight in the law of God after the inward man:*
> *But I see another law in my members,*
> *warring against the law of my mind,*
> *and bringing me into captivity to the law of sin*
> *which is in my members.*[2]

Paul is trying to describe a spiritual being who loves God and wills that good happen but who also is trapped by the base qualities of his own flesh. The admirable qualities represent our identity (our eternally true identity) before we were ever born on Earth. The qualities we have no admiration for are those of the matter of Earth itself, the matter out of which our bodies are made. The qualities of matter are a prison from which we must eventually escape. In this escape we will transform the prison into a garden.

---

[2] Rom. 7:18–23.

## A Perspective on Duality

Most of us are familiar with orthodox Christian teachings on the state of duality. To oversimplify: you are full of sin (selfish qualities) until you open your life, your heart, and mind to a savior (Christ) who saves you through his action. You do the best you can here on Earth and when you die you get a great reward for being faithful to the doctrine and the Savior. Your great reward is eternal life, in a state of grace and goodness at the side of the Father. Through this process, you move from the totally sinful, temporal state to the sinless, eternal state by following certain recommendations faithfully. In this way, one travels the full spectrum of duality.

Using one of the parables Christ used, the prodigal son,[3] we can take another perspective on the problem of duality. As the parable goes, the son leaves his father's house, goes to live in the world, and becomes lost in it. The son immerses himself in every human diversion and perversion. He is gone so long that he completely forgets about his father. The son eventually tires of the ways of the world and thinks again of the wonderful life with his father. He remembers the way back and returns. His return enormously pleases his father.

This parable is full of implications. If you take yourself to be the prodigal son, this parable infers that you had an existence with the Father that preceded your life on Earth. For some reason, you left the Father's side and came to live on Earth. What could possibly cause you to leave the exalted state of life in the Father's house? What could cause you to trade immortality for mortality and bliss for pain?

---
[3] Luke 15:11–32.

When we live with the Father, we are surrounded with the purpose for the creation and its unfoldment in time and space. We don't just know the purpose, we are dedicated to it, we breathe it, we become it. Therefore, it is unlikely that we chose to come to Earth to start a life separated from the Father just for fun or out of a teenage rebellion. Only the impelling, irresistible purpose of the Father could cause us to do so.

The Father's House

We leave the Father's house impelled by the Father's purpose

Each of us must become the Way of return

Spiritual Worlds ▲

Material Worlds ▼

We are called to return and we spiritualize the world by releasing the saving force

We encase ourselves in matter

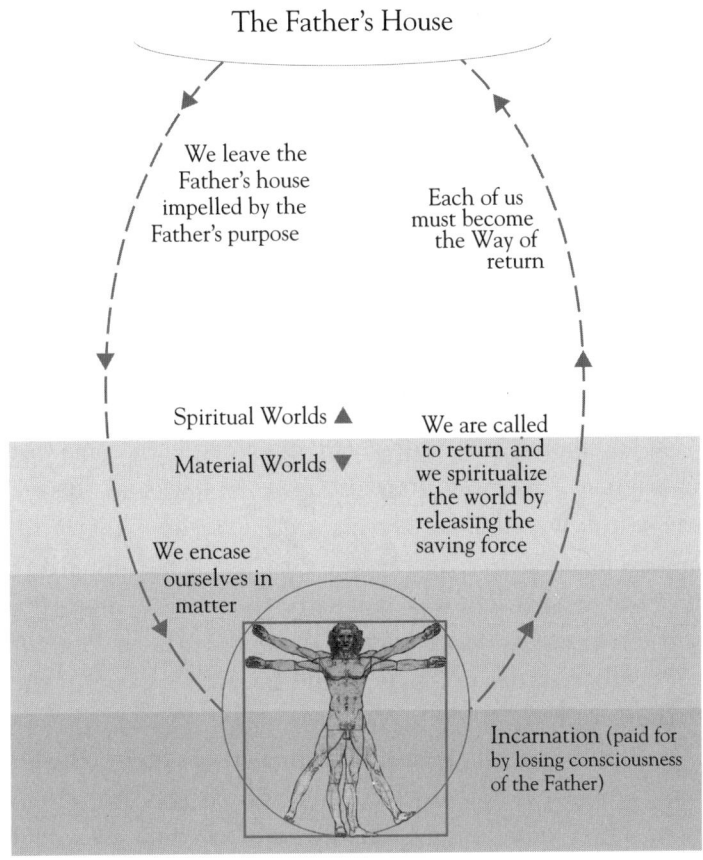

Incarnation (paid for by losing consciousness of the Father)

*Figure 1-1. The Prodigal Son*

From that high perspective at the side of the Father, we would have known what we were getting ourselves into. We left knowing that being born on Earth meant that we would have a life separated (at least in consciousness) from the Father. Before we left the Father, we would have had some sense of the pain, loneliness, hardship, and degradation of life on Earth. The only worthy purpose for coming to live on Earth was to *save* it. We came as heroes with the express purpose of saving the world. The Father needed us to go, and we went, knowing the price. The price was forgetting our lives at the side of the Father and living our earthly lives in separation from the Father. In separation, we lost our way and our sense of true identity. Immersed in the world, we became the world. We traded love for selfishness and lost the divine light in the darkness and heaviness of Earth. We exchanged eternal life for death. True death is not the death of our physical body; it is becoming imprisoned by the matter of Earth. We chose death in Earth to save it. We chose separation from the Father to create a greater unity.

Our coming here is no accident. We did not come just by chance. And more than just a special few came to save the world. We all came as a giant group to save the world. We came together, in response to the same impelling purpose. In this light we can see that the whole of humanity is the true prodigal son, leaving the Father's house not out of rebellion or desire for the world but rather to fulfill the Father's will.

We will eventually return to the Father's house. We all have one tiny strand of connection to the Father no matter how far from the Father we are. Without it, we would stop thinking, feeling, moving, and breathing. While we are not always conscious of this thread, it forms the basis of our consciousness of the Father. This thread of connection shows itself in our conscience. It also causes our admiration of the qualities of the hero/savior. If you have any admiration for good, any hope that good will happen, then rest assured that some impulse is coming down this thread from the Father's house. You have immersed yourself as far into matter as you need to, and you have received the call to work your way back.

*Man's main task in life is to give birth to himself.*
ERICH FROMM

Many of us find ourselves today still stuck in materiality, exhibiting material qualities yet touched by a sense of great goodness. Most of us have passed the farthest point from the Father's house and are returning. This return is the consummation of our original mission. We came here to save Earth. Earth is so dense and thickly imbued with the qualities of matter that it can be saved only from the inside out. Our mission, our purpose, was to pay the price and come to Earth in human form. In the depths of our material existence, we were to respond to the call of the Father. In responding, we become tiny points of reception of the Father's qualities while we are alive in the material world.

We don't just push the matter out of our way and go home. Going home is a long process in which we progressively free the Father's saving force. The saving force redeems, transforms, and spiritualizes the matter of Earth. The saving force enlivens and quickens the slowness of matter and enlightens the darkness of matter. It brings awareness where there was none. It changes coldness to warmth, hate to love, instinct to wisdom, and selfishness to the sacrificial purpose of the Father.

The saving force irrevocably changes the matter of the world, the physical, emotional, and mental matter into which we took human form. We act as conduits for the qualities of the Father. These qualities redeem the three grades of matter. The matter of the world is forever different for our having passed through it, and the Father's plan to save the world moves further toward fulfillment.

We leave the Father's house together, and we will return together, but not all simultaneously. This fact is what is so confusing about life on Earth. While we are all traveling together in the process of leaving and returning to the Father's house, we are all at different points. Some of our group have already returned. Our brother, whom many call Christ, was the first of our group to make it back. Being the first of us to free the saving force, he holds a special relationship with all of us. He is the prototype of the return. He became the Way of return. He, however, did not save and is not saving the world in place of us. Each of us still has to become the Way ourselves, in concert with the Father, just as he did.

# 2

# *Redemption:*
## *The Spiritualization of Matter*

> **redeem**, *vt*. **1 a :** to buy back **:** REPURCHASE **b :** to get or win back **2 a :** to liberate by payment **:** RANSOM **b :** to free by force **:** LIBERATE **c :** to release from blame or debt **:** CLEAR **d :** to free from the consequences of sin **3 :** to change for the better **:** REFORM **4 :** REPAIR, RESTORE **5 :** FULFILL **6 a :** EXPIATE **b :** RETRIEVE
>
> WEBSTER'S SEVENTH NEW COLLEGIATE DICTIONARY

We may not recognize it as such, but we spend our lives redeeming the world. What is redemption and how do we redeem? The general theme is paying a price to rescue or save, to bring to a better or higher state. What are we trying to bring to a higher state and what is the price? Many of us believe that the focus of redemption is the saving of ourselves. In truth, what we need to be saved from is the illusion that *we* need to be saved. Our bodies, feelings, and minds need to be saved, but they are just our vehicles of expression; they are made of the stuff of Earth. We did not seek to be born into the matter of Earth so that we would be saved. We were already in a state that did not need saving before we made that decision. We chose birth here to save the world. It is the world that we are spiritualizing—bringing to a higher spiritual state.

What is the world? Certainly it includes the physical world, the spinning sphere of rock, water, and air. Certainly it includes the plants, animals, and human bodies. But the world includes more and, we have to admit, more than we know. The world is made of grades of matter that are quite gross and evident but also grades of matter that are so fine and rarefied that we are totally unaware of them. We have chosen to inhabit the grosser matter of Earth, and we have paid a heavy price for that choice. The price is the loss of our conscious connection to our home and our identity in the rarefied worlds—the worlds we now call the spiritual realms.

We chose birth into the physical world, and we inhabit bodies made of physical matter. But we simultaneously chose birth into two more worlds, the emotional and mental worlds. These worlds are also made of matter but a matter so much less gross than physical matter that we do not tend to think of it as matter at all. However, when we consider this kind of matter, it proves to have the same general characteristics as physical matter.

Take emotions, for example. Places and people seem to have emotional atmospheres surrounding them. Think of (and feel) the difference in the emotional atmospheres at Mardi Gras, a funeral home, and a chemistry classroom. Think of the emotional atmosphere surrounding a woman finding she has the winning lottery numbers, as opposed to a man finding out he has only six months to live. Anyone in these atmospheres cannot help feeling them. The woman winning the lottery generates a powerful feeling of elation.

The atmosphere of elation touches everyone around her and is so obvious as to be nearly tangible. These atmospheres are of another world and that world is made out of stuff, subtle stuff, but stuff. The emotional world becomes even more tangible and real if we make the physical world temporarily go away, as we do in dreaming. In our dreams, the world is still there, but it is much less solid. We still have experiences involving people, places, and things, but time and space seem more fluid. Whatever we imagine happens.

In the emotional world, grades of density correspond to the grades of density of physical matter. We can easily tell the difference in "density" of a feeling of sadness as opposed to a feeling of joy. Sadness "weighs" more than joy; it is more dense, more solid. The more dense emotions are those of fear, depression, jealousy, greed, and hate. The less dense emotions are those of aspiration and happiness.

Just as in the physical world, in the emotional world we have a "body" that we use to exist, sense, and work. We commonly call this body our feelings. It has many characteristics of the physical body. We think of it as our own. We get our feelings hurt, just as we get our physical bodies hurt. Just as in the physical world where some of us are more accomplished with our bodies (for example, athletes), some of us seem to have greater facility with our emotions than do others of us.

The other world we inhabit is the mental world. This world is even more rarefied than the emotional world. To get a sense of the relative density of these three worlds, we could compare them to the three states of matter: solid, liquid, and gaseous. If the physical world corresponds to the solid state and the emotional world corresponds to the liquid state, then the mental world corresponds to the gaseous state. Even in the physical world we have trouble seeing gas and vapors, and in the same way the mental world is much less "visible" and evident. Most of us fit right into the physical and emotional worlds, but we need some introduction and training to feel at home in the mental world. The purpose of our educational system is to help us exercise and develop our mental faculties.

Spiritual Worlds ▲

Material Worlds ▼

Mental World (analogous to the gaseous state) — Mind

Emotional World (analogous to the liquid state) — Feelings — Personal Self

Physical World (analogous to the solid state) — Body

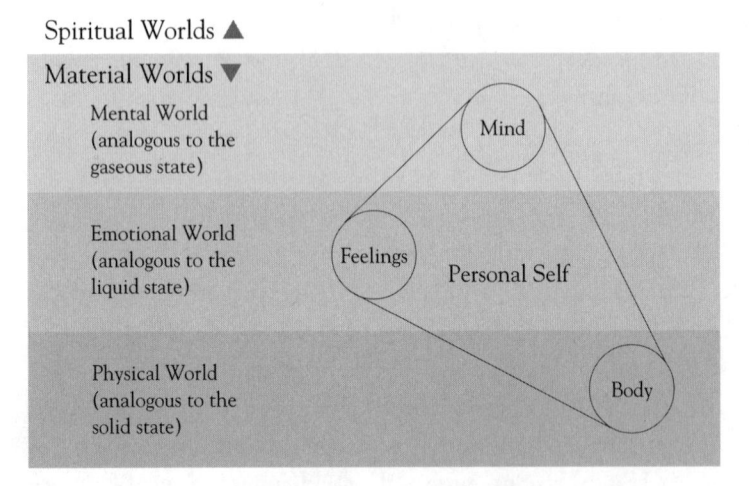

*Figure 2-1. The three worlds, the three vehicles (or bodies), and the personal self.*

As in the physical and emotional worlds, each of us also has a "body" that we use in the mental world. We call this body our mind. Please note the difference between the brain, an organ in the physical world, and the mind, our "body" in the mental world. The mind is not merely a function of the brain. The reverse is more true. The brain is the physical expression of the mind. If no thinker is present, the brain occupies itself with sensory and motor activity. We think in the mind, not the brain. The mind is the writer/producer/broadcaster, while the brain is the television set receiving and displaying the mind's signal.

The mental world is divided. The denser part is the rational or concrete mental world, while the more rarefied part is the abstract mental world. Our mental body is similarly divided into the logical mind and the abstract mind. As you might expect, most of us have more facility and experience with the logical mind than we do with the abstract mind.

The mental world is also made of stuff, mind stuff or *chitta*, as Patanjali, author of the *Yoga Sutras*, named it 6,000 years ago. We take formless, abstract mental stuff and form it into mental objects we experience as thoughts. We can make new ones or trade ones we have already made between ourselves. We also use the mind to reason and to learn the effects of our actions, feelings, and thoughts.

We have chosen to be born into or to "take bodies" in these three worlds. We chose this drastic step because each of these worlds is characterized by qualities that do not allow the intention of the Creator to shine forth in all its glory. These worlds are displaying somewhat the Creator's intelligence, but they are not yet displaying his love. Humanity is part of the team sent here to bring love to life. Among the many qualities of love are the general qualities of attraction, relation, and inclusion. Redemption means releasing the matter of these three worlds from their present qualities and enhancing it with the qualities of love.

## Redeeming in the Physical World

So how do we redeem? How do we spiritualize matter? In the physical world, redemption is such an innate part of ourselves that we do much of it quite naturally and unconsciously. Physical redemption is upgrading the quality of the stuff of the physical world—the atoms, the chemicals, the objects.

For example, think about two people you know. Make sure that these people have very different qualities. Think about each of them moving into identical houses on the same date. Then think how those houses would be after ten years. They would no longer be identical. The appearance, the character, the feel, the condition would be quite different. The different qualities of the people caused the differences in the houses. In understanding redemption, it is not the differences that are important but rather the fact that the people changed the houses at all. The qualities of the people eventually showed themselves to some extent in the houses. And it was not just the houses that picked up the qualities. The people changed the quality of the matter, the atoms that make up the houses.

Admittedly, it is an unusual concept to think that we have any effect on atoms. It is easy to see our effect on the house, while changing the quality of atoms seems a bit far-fetched. In one sense atoms are as distant from us as galaxies. They are not visible to the naked eye, and we must rely on a concept of atoms created by science that leaves us thinking they are generic, identical, and unchanging. At this point it is more than fair to ask, "Even if we can change the qualities of atoms, what qualities are we talking about, and why is that at all important?" The explanation is somewhat complicated, requiring more than a few words.

The matter of Earth has certain qualities. These are mechanical qualities (density, hardness, flexibility), chemical qualities (bond strength, pH), and electromagnetic qualities (resistance, polarity). These qualities reflect the basic divine principle of intelligence. We are so accustomed to the way matter is that it is difficult to imagine that matter formerly did not have these basic qualities. But let's make the assumption that matter was once totally without intelligence. It did not know how to stay together, respond to gravity, interact chemically or electrically, combust, or ionize; it was completely stupid. Total chaos would exist on the atomic level. (Actually there would not even be atoms.) This stage is referred to in Genesis:

*In the beginning...the earth was without form.* [4]

Let's also assume that matter did not become intelligent by some random chance. Let's assume that matter "learned" to be intelligent by an eons-long association with a grand, intelligent Being and his workers. The term "learn" refers to what human beings do. Humans are active, but matter is passive; matter does not really learn in the same sense humans do. Matter became imbued with intelligence through association, through a relationship with that grand intelligence, the Creator. On a tiny scale, the two people moving into the identical houses acted as the grand intelligences for the atoms of the houses. The atoms of the houses were in some degree changed through those relationships.

[4] Gen. 1:1–2.

Every physical piece of the planet that we eat, drink, breathe, wear, use, visit, or associate with comes into a physical relationship with us. Through this relationship and association we spiritualize and save the matter of the physical world. By just our presence, we change the quality of the matter in our physical environment. As we have a meal or talk on the telephone, the spiritual qualities of intelligence and love flow through each of us and "color" the matter we contact. Is it a dramatic change? Usually it's not. It's more like water wearing away rock. But over time you could have the Grand Canyon.

It is interesting to consider the amazing volumes of stuff that you have physically related to over your lifetime. For example, breathing normally over an eighty-year lifetime, we will breathe a volume of air equivalent to 550 to 850 average-size houses. Over a lifetime, we drink and eat the volume of an average-size house. Think of the objects, plants, animals, and people you have touched. Some things stay for a long time, some come and go quickly, but all are imbued with a little of your qualities of intelligence and love, forever.

How does the quality of love show itself through an atom? Certainly through magnetism, gravity, and other expressions of attractiveness, the lowest quality of love. Higher qualities of love like compassion and wisdom are going to be more difficult to see yet because we are generally not that far along in bringing them to life *in our own lives*. We are very active and intelligent, but love is only beginning to blossom in humankind. We can radiate only the qualities we live. It is this radiation that colors matter. It is this enrichment with the qualities of the Creator that redeems matter and saves it from the prison of what it was.

Most of our redemptive work in the physical world is unconscious. Yet we can work consciously. Working consciously is like putting redemption into hyperdrive. Just realizing that we are participating in this project is a good start. That realization is like turning on the lights in a dark room we had been stumbling around in forever.

Physical redemption is the basis of the religious activity of blessing. Religions encourage us to bless our food, our homes, and each other. Many of us consider objects blessed or worn by great souls to be holy. Great, unexplained healings occur by touch. All this is but the recognition that we give something of a spiritual nature to matter through the miracle of presence, the miracle of touch.

## REDEEMING IN THE EMOTIONAL WORLD

While our work with the physical stuff of Earth is important, our redemptive work with the world of emotions is even more important. Humans are generally quite busy in the emotional world. All of us have had the experience of being in a serene emotional state until a person who is angry comes into our presence. Even if he or she does not direct anger at us, it is so easy to be invaded by and react to it. This is especially true if we have some resonant anger lurking inside us. We attract feelings. We draw them to us like moths to a light.

A useful symbol of this process is the vortex. We pull feelings, emotions, and aspirations into our lives, hold on to them for a while, and then send them off. As they circulate through our lives, we temporarily "become" them. We speak of this identification when we say "I am angry!"

Becoming what we will redeem is the first step in the process. The next step is to imbue the emotion of anger with our essential nature (love). We "get over it" and send it out as love instead of anger. Our interaction with it has forever changed the emotional stuff. Because we made the hard choice of love in the face of anger, that little "volume" of emotional stuff will not now present the challenge of hate to any others. If other humans can attract love, they can draw that little bit of redeemed anger to them as love.

Identifying with emotions

Attracting unredeemed emotions

Releasing redeemed emotions

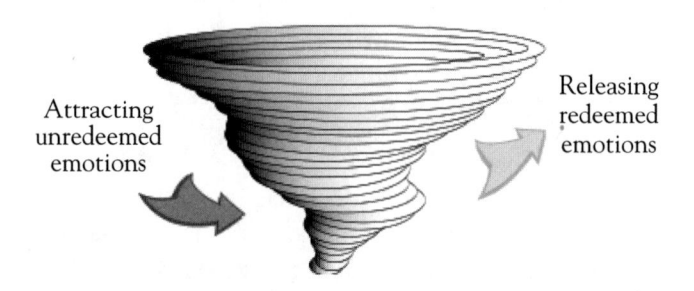

Figure 2-2. *The emotional body as a vortex of redemption. We work in a similar manner in the mental and physical worlds.*

We do our redemptive work in the physical world mostly unconsciously. Unfortunately, we also redeem mostly unconsciously in the emotional world, and this has led to problems. We draw the negative, unredeemed emotions like anger, jealousy, and irritation to us mostly through ignorance. We become these emotions. Up to this point, everything is going according to plan. The problem comes when we send an emotion back out into the world. If we have not sanctified and redeemed an emotion, we send it back out into the world as it originally was, only more highly charged. When it came to us it was anger; when we send it back out, it is anger plus. And because it has been so recently in a human system, it is highly "infectious" to other humans. Nothing multiplies like anger in a crowd.

So while we have much work to do in the physical world, we have even more to do in the emotional world. Note that we have been adding to the problem in the emotional world. We not only have to redeem what was present when we first started on this huge project of redemption, but now we also have to redeem what we have been "unredeeming" in the process all these many years. The bad news is that we have quite a backlog. The good news is that we can do it.

Redeeming in the emotional world is not easy. For most of us, emotions, feelings, and desires are quite compelling. All of us have had the experience of waking up a little tired or edgy or irritated. It is surprising sometimes to see what comes out of us the first time someone throws a negative emotion our way; it is usually not a thing of beauty. If we consciously keep our emotional natures serene and sweet, we greatly enhance our powers of redemption. If our feelings are themselves swirling with negativity, they react more easily to negative emotions in our environment.

A confusing situation has challenged us all. Let's say that we are in the throes of a strong, negative emotion. We know it is wrong to continue; we want to stop and redeem it, but we just can't. Two well-known schools of thought offer advice for such a dilemma. One says to put on a happy face, even if you are still harboring ill will inside, and go on about your business. The other school says never suppress your feelings; always express them. Get them out in the open; if you are angry about something, show it.

It seems that neither of these methods redeems the negative emotion. At best, they only make us feel better. We can never redeem an emotional problem on the level of the emotions. We can solve this problem only by taking a perspective that allows us to release our identification with the emotion. Whether you say you are angry or not, whether you act out your anger or not, you can never redeem the anger if you are still angry. The perspective that the mind can give will allow you to lose your identification and do your job. If we take the identity of a cool and calm mental observer of our emotions, the emotions become things. We have the power to redeem a thing. We have the power to change it into something much better than what it is. In that calm and thoughtful state, we can remember love and our purpose for being and begin to understand and sincerely forgive.

Many techniques can be used to become the observer, like the famous method of counting to ten or taking a deep breath. All of them work so much better if we know what we are doing and work at it consciously. What makes taking the identity of the observer so difficult is waiting until we have fully given our identity to anger or self-pity. Seeking to switch identities in the midst of an emotional crisis can seem impossible at the time. If we routinely take the perspective of the observer and routinely observe our emotions, it gets far easier to do.

I once made an agreement to observe the emotion of irritation in myself for one month. Up until then, I had an image of myself as one who does not get irritated. To my surprise, I found that I got irritated quite a bit. I started by merely realizing when I had already become irritated. That observation helped me remember that my identity was not irritation and I could stop. When I recovered, I would retrace my steps through my path of emotional destruction, caring for the wounded and asking for forgiveness.

As the month progressed, I got better at catching irritation earlier in the process. The earlier I caught it, the easier it was to deal with. Then the most interesting thing happened. I could see a situation arising that would surely make me irritated. I went into the situation as the mental observer, keeping my head out of the emotional waters. When the irritation "invaded" me, I had the fortune to observe it as a scientist would. I saw what in me caused it to come. I felt it enter and felt the physiology it provoked. I saw its nature, which only one word could describe: ugly. I had been so busy *being* irritation before then, I had never noticed how ugly and unwholesome it really was. I also had never noticed that irritation is a thing, a thing that we make out of emotional matter. We freely trade these creations, perhaps the sickest of our creations, back and forth between ourselves.

Working consciously is so much more efficient and productive than working unconsciously. We do not have to compound the problem by feeling bad about becoming low-grade emotional states since that is part of the spiritualization of matter. We cannot fully redeem without becoming what needs to be redeemed. If we are not aware that an emotion needs redemption, we can be swept along being the low-grade emotion for far too long, creating more work for ourselves. When we become aware of the fact that we are redeemers, we can swiftly, elegantly and beautifully spiritualize low-grade emotions and color them with our natural state of love. Awareness in our work draws the strength of our original sacrificial purpose. We can call on this strength to draw the Creator's power (in a small way) to spiritualize particularly difficult emotions.

Redeeming emotions is difficult work, but we have much help. Many redeemers have passed this way before us and knew the true purpose of "turning the other cheek." They knew that reacting to a negative emotion with a negative emotion only escalates the problem and piles up the work to do. They knew that reacting to a negative emotion with wisdom and understanding changes it forever. They knew that when they faced the difficulty of transforming the negative emotion, it could no longer infect others with its negativity. Transforming a tiny bit of the emotional world makes it easier for love to live purely in all our hearts and to share with each other.

## Redeeming in the Mental World

The very nature of the mental world makes the job there quite different. We have done far less damage in the mental world than we have in the emotional world and have less mess of our own making to clean up. That is because we spend far less time in the mental world and are not yet as powerful on that level of existence as we are in the emotional world.

We use the mental world correctly much of the time, in the sense that we take chaotic, irrational, disordered thoughts and bring a logical order to them. This is the process we use to program a videocassette recorder using the sometimes unclear instructions that come in the box. We take problems and figure them out. The use of the mind also allows us to create physical forms, and we have surely taken advantage of that faculty. The mind is the vehicle we use to reduce ideas to thoughts and thoughts to words and other symbols and thereby communicate with each other. Another use of the mind is to understand the relationship of cause and effect. While we are somewhat limited in tracing cause back to its ultimate originating source, we are using this faculty to learn about the universe and its natural laws.

The concrete, rational mind is a powerful organ for making divisions and drawing distinctions. We use it to isolate, name, and classify. The abstract mind is a powerful organ for seeing how all the parts fit into the whole. Used together, the whole mind can be an amazing instrument for promoting good.

One of our biggest problems is that we hardly ever use the whole mind. When we use the lower mind alone, the world appears to be divided and the parts unrelated. We erroneously perceive deep divisions among people, races, religions, nations, and political systems. When we use discrimination in a strictly personal, egotistic sense, it can become a weapon we use against each other. Locked in our discriminative faculty, we erroneously perceive the final division, the division between God and ourselves. God can seem distant or nonexistent. When selfishness rules our lives and uses the discriminative faculty as its servant, we have the critical, judgmental person. At present this is the predominant human situation: a well-developed physical and emotional nature with a moderately developed concrete mind and a slightly developed abstract mind. This combination provides the foundation for a strong sense of self-identity and a passionately critical nature.

Discrimination is already a quality of matter. Birds know which seeds to eat and which not to eat. Plants pull only certain compounds into their systems, rejecting many others. A chemical is attracted to certain chemicals but not to others. Discrimination is a method of separation, and we use it to distinguish ourselves from others. We also use it to distinguish the qualities that need to be redeemed from the ones that don't.

Criticism comes so naturally to most of us. We can be critical of our own selves, but the faults of others are usually glaringly evident, especially when they offend us in some way. Our critical nature allows us to say "He has bad qualities; I am not like him." Often that critical thought leads to a separation. We think that since some people are so bad and so offensive, they could not be in our group; they must be in some other group especially for people that bad.

Revulsion to the unredeemed qualities in others is the basis of the many divisions arising within humanity. Many times this revulsion is why family members sever relations and people get fired or quit their jobs in disgust. Often, revulsion is why neighbors and members of churches don't speak with each other. It is why many of us get divorced and quarrel with our friends. It is the basis of racism, sexism, nationalism, and, in the extreme, war of all kinds.

*It is easier to discover a deficiency*
*in individuals, in states, and in Providence,*
*than to see their real import and value.*
GEORG WILHEIM HEGEL

Criticism is a natural faculty and we need it to tell redeemed from unredeemed qualities. But how can we live with this faculty and not let it cause divisions between us? I made the case in the previous section that we can never solve the problem of an emotion on the level of the emotions. We have to get up into the mind and take on the cool, collected identity of the observer to lose our identity with the emotion and then successfully spiritualize it. This same technique won't work with criticism because it is a concrete mental function. When we criticize, we are already in the mind. Being in the mind, we can securely rationalize our position against the offensive person, which only makes the situation worse.

Fortunately a higher faculty than the mind exists. Using this higher faculty we can take a perspective on the criticism, lose our identification with it, and redeem it. This higher faculty is the soul. The word "soul" has so many meanings and connotations that an explanation would help.

In chapter 1 we use the story of the prodigal son to intimate that we used to live with the Father. Later we chose to live on Earth, forgetting our former existence. That gives us the sense that we packed our bags, filled out our change-of-address cards, and moved out of the Father's house. The truth is we never left, or we could say that part of us never left. The absolute, eternal core of our being is still with the Father. We can call this essential core of our existence the spiritual man, or simply the spirit. The spirit never left the Father but chose to project itself into the three worlds (mental, emotional, physical). The intended result of this projection is a person, an agent of redemption of those three worlds. Another result is a serious communication problem. The Father's home and the three human worlds are so different that they have trouble relating to each other. As is evident to most of us, we seem to have very little face-to-face time with God. He is with us, but we mostly don't recognize it. However, to some degree or another, a relationship exists between our spiritual self and our earthly self. We name that relationship the soul. The soul is the divine intermediary, the Way, the middle principle.

We call it the Way because it is the way that God's life, love, and intelligence find expression through our bodies, hearts, and minds. We call it the Way because it is the way a person lost in the world returns to the life of the spirit. We all have a soul; we do not have to earn it. We take the steps on the Way mostly by giving up. What we give up is

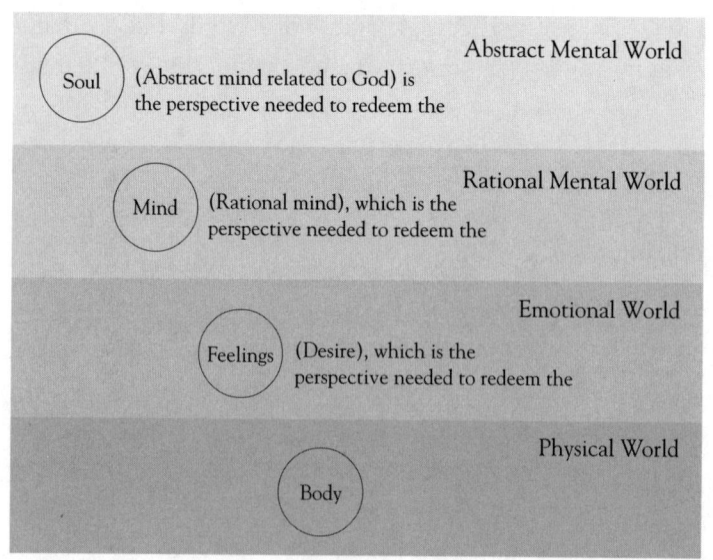

Abstract Mental World
Soul (Abstract mind related to God) is the perspective needed to redeem the

Rational Mental World
Mind (Rational mind), which is the perspective needed to redeem the

Emotional World
Feelings (Desire), which is the perspective needed to redeem the

Physical World
Body

Figure 2-3. *Conscious redemption of each of our "bodies" requires taking a perspective of a higher body.*

our outworn identities and our attachments to the allurements of the three worlds.

The soul is the higher identity into which we can retreat to break our identity with the critical mind. The soul is the basis of brotherhood, and through the eyes of the soul we can get a glimpse of the divine intention that inspires the project in which we are all playing our part. We still use the discriminative nature to see the distinctions between the redeemed qualities and those that need redemption. We see the members of humanity working together yet all working at different steps and stages. When we identify with the critical mind, we can call some of these workers evil, sinful, or unworthy. Through the eyes of the soul we see our spiritual brothers entranced and imprisoned by the grittier, tougher qualities of matter. We see that they are just doing their job of redeeming matter at that level. The matter needs redemption, and the redeemers are our brothers and sisters. We have compassion for their plight. We realize why we must not judge each other. We naturally reach out to them to help in some way because we realize that we would be helping the whole divine project.

# 3

# *Why It Is So Difficult*

*The world is hard to love, though we must love it
because we have no other,
and to fail to love it is not to exist at all.*
MARK VAN DOREN

Saving the world is difficult for many reasons. For one, we are redeeming matter, and the properties of matter create great resistance to spiritualization. One of the properties of matter is inertia, the tendency to not change. Physicists define inertia as the tendency of matter at rest to remain at rest and of matter in motion to remain in motion. Inertia is why we have to work to heave a rock and why it keeps going after we throw it. It also means that much energy is needed to make any kind of change in the world, but once an idea or program starts to happen, it is difficult to stop it or change it. Other properties of matter are heaviness and darkness. These properties tend to overwhelm us. Matter is so dark and heavy that we tend to lose ourselves in the material world. The heaviness of materiality stuns us at birth, and we usually lose all sense of our true selves and our purpose for being born. Matter is so heavy and thick that it acts as more of a prison than a home. Another property of matter is separativeness. The world looks divided through material eyes. We seem to be totally separate from each other. I seem to stop right here, and you seem to start over there, with nothing connecting us.

Another reason saving the world is difficult is the inherent problems of redemption. In the midst of our encumbering materiality, we are supposed to awaken to our true nature and transform the world. A task of that scope is just not that easy. It takes a long time to get the slightest notion that at our core we are spiritual beings and to get even a glimpse of our redemptive purpose. We have to do much of our work here with no more to go on than partial truths, faith, and fleeting glimmers of reality. This limited vision causes us to make so many errors. It is understandable that we would make errors while we are identified with selfishness, but even when we begin to act as conscious redeemers, we make errors. A slight brush with truth sets us on fire, and often in the name of goodness we tear at each other mentally, emotionally, and physically. And errors cause pain, awesome physical and emotional pain. Pain seems unbearable at times, but it teaches us lessons that are difficult to learn any other way.

Still another reason it is difficult to save the world is the sheer scale of the undertaking. The world is so big. The problems are so complicated, and we are so small and so powerless. A tiny glimmer of what world problems would look like if they were solved throws into relief the enormous amount of change needed. We are busy redeeming the problems in our own lives. How can we redeem world-sized problems of injustice, brutality, hate, crime, and war?

It seems that no one person could make a dent in world problems. The only way to make any progress would be if we could all pull together. But realistically, what are the chances of that? Much of our society seems to run on the juices of selfishness, greed, and competition. Enormous walls separate the people of different religions. A vast economic chasm separates the very rich and the very poor. Nation stands against nation and race against race.

## The Trance of Materiality

A story tells of a demented king who chose to spend much of his life in a dark dungeon under his castle. In losing his mind, he could not remember the glorious life he had in the kingdom only a few feet above his cell. He thought his cell was his kingdom and the roaches and the rats were his subjects. No one could convince him otherwise.

In the darkness, heaviness, half-truths, and pain of the material world we live our lives in much the same way. Like the king, we have lost the sense of our true selves. We have become entranced by our materiality. We have made our own little kingdom based on the separative nature of matter. It is the kingdom of materiality, and it gets its power from an illusion: if you can't know something through the senses, it doesn't exist. Many of us think of our material life as the only possible life. We symbolize that perspective in the phrase "that is what really *matters*." If it is not material, it is not important. In our trance, matter is the measure of existence.

Many of us believe that we cannot exist without our physical body. Many of us sincerely believe that we are one-dimensional, that we are only physical. Some of us believe that our existence sprang from nothing more than a random combination of atoms. Many scientists working in neurobiology believe that our whole lives, every thought, feeling, and insight, are mere chemistry taking place in our brains. They refuse to believe that anything subtler than the physical life exists.

> *Our soul is cast into a body, where it finds number, time, dimension. Thereupon it reasons, and calls this nature necessity, and can believe nothing else.*
> BLAISE PASCAL

These perspectives are common because of the heaviness and slowness of matter. When we are born into a physical body it is like being dropped into a vat of thick, dark oil. We can't sense very well nor move very fast. Our material eyes are so slow and dense that we can only see what is right in front of us, and we lose sight of the quick, rare worlds of the spirit. We seem to be alone, separated from the Creator and each other.

In materiality, the instincts to survive and avoid pain are the driving forces in our lives, and we quickly learn the ways of the material world. Comfort and security are prized, and we learn what we must do to get them. Whatever brings comfort is attractive to us, and we tend to repeat it seemingly without end. This sets up the patterns and habits of our lives and, in the extreme, our addictions. Through these habits we try to insure our comfort, but eventually they become our prisons. We take our bodies, instincts, habits, sentiments, and thoughts to be ourselves. We become our materiality.

Breaking the trance of materiality happens through a series of recognitions. Slowly, we begin to recognize that our physical bodies, feelings (emotional bodies), and minds (mental bodies) are material in nature. Eventually, we recognize that each of these is a projection of our spiritual self into the three worlds (physical, emotional, and mental) that we inhabit. Each of these projections is a vehicle for the expression of an aspect of our spiritual selves. The physical body expresses the intelligence aspect. The emotional body expresses the love aspect. The mental body

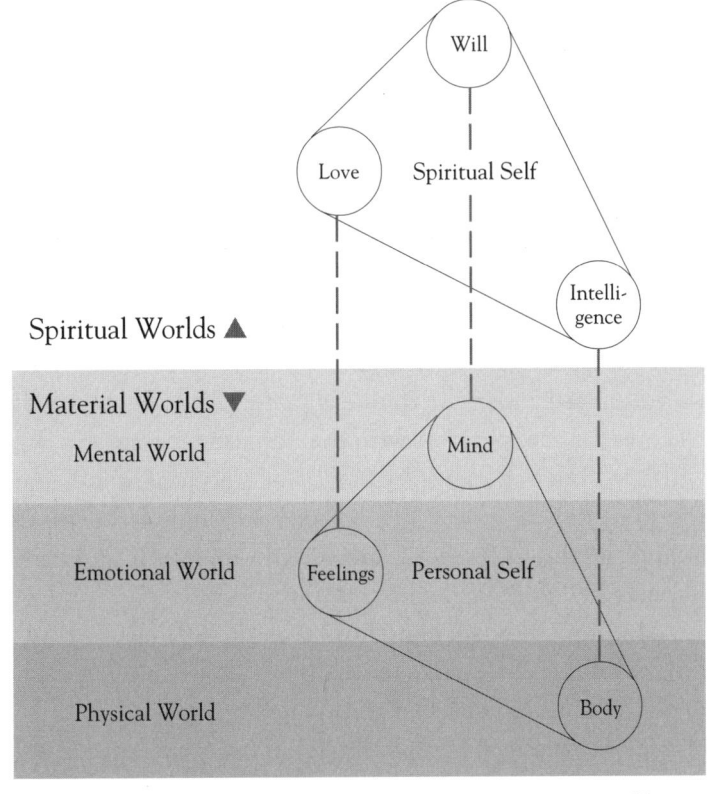

*Figure 3-1. Projection of the spiritual self into the three worlds.*

expresses the will aspect. Our spiritual self is the three aspects taken as a whole, while our personal self is the three vehicles taken as a whole. When connected consciously, the spiritual self has four vehicles at its disposal: the physical body, the emotions, the mind, and the personality, the synthesis of the other three. (See figure 3-1.)

We all must go through a somewhat long process of identifying with one vehicle after another. We first think of ourselves as the physical body. At some point we recognize that we have a physical body but that we are not our physical body. Many of us are recognizing that we have feelings and emotions but that they are not who we are. Feeling becomes a function, not an identity. Others of us are recognizing the same is true of our minds. We have thoughts, but we are not our thoughts. The thinker is not the thought nor the vehicle of thought, the mind.

Maybe the most difficult recognition to make is that we are not at all material, that we are not even personalities. But just as surely as we have made those previous recognitions, we will recognize that we have a personality and that we are not a personality. When we recognize that, we will have broken the trance of materiality. Then we will be conscious cooperators with the purpose for creation. We will have four vehicles (physical body, emotions, mind, and the personality) at our disposal for redeeming the three densest worlds of the creation. We can then fully and consciously free the saving force into the world.

Making these recognitions is most difficult but not impossible, and we will eventually set about doing it, each in our own unique way. Each one of us who breaks the trance of our own materiality makes it easier for the next one and the next.

## The World We Made

Recognizing that we are in the world but not of the world will take quite a while. Yet all through this process we have been creating our own world. The concept that we are creators may be confusing. Certainly we are not creating the whole world, but we are prolific creators. The faculty of creation seems to be shared among many life forms. The nests of animals are examples of a low-grade, rather unconscious creation. However, it is in humankind that the Creator increasingly shares creative power. It is true that we are not yet entrusted with full creative power. Until we get over our selfishness, that would be too dangerous.

We do know the rudiments of creation. Whether we are going to create a chair or a multinational corporation, the process is generally the same. We start with a purpose or have a vision. We create a plan to fulfill the vision. We harmonize the plan with what is truly possible. We experiment, test, and figure out what works. We devote the resources necessary. We organize it all into a creation. To the Creator, this probably sounds like a two-year-old reciting his ABCs, but we have used this method to create our great cities; our health, educational, economic, communication, and transportation systems; our societies, governments, arts, philosophies, sciences, and technologies of all description. Animals make their lives cozier with nests, but we have created our own world.

It stands to reason that the world we created would be less than perfect. After all, the creators are a bit confused. Generally, we take ourselves to be personalities and we are unaware of any grand mission that we must fulfill. Personalities are generally unconcerned with the big picture and more concerned with their own lives, wants, and beliefs. Personalities spend most of their lives trying to fulfill their wants. They want to be comfortable, satisfied, adored, rich, and powerful.

No wonder the world we made reflects the wishes of our personalities. It is a world where we no longer just eat; we dine on the finest and rarest morsels. It is a world where we don't just clothe and shelter ourselves; our homes and clothes must make a statement about us and how much money we control. It is a world of rapid rises and falls of fashions, styles, and fads. It is a world of seeking fame, with one after another of us taking our turn in the spotlight, only to quickly lose it. It is a world where some of us exercise power over others for no other reason than to increase our own status or bank account or simply for the thrill of it.

It is a world where we seem to be free, but are we? Many of us are learning the stinging lessons of mistaking license for freedom with little regard to responsibility and consequences. Crime flourishes, as does incarceration. Outright slavery still exists in our world. Economic slavery is the rule, not the exception. We are not free from human rights violations, nor are we free from excesses of cruelty and torture. Most of us are still slaves to our own wants.

It is a world of divisions. An enormous gulf separates the rich and the poor. The rich minority is living virtually on a different planet from the poor majority. An astronomical difference divides the two groups in their access to material comforts, nutrition, healthcare, technology, and educational opportunities. We divide ourselves all too easily along racial, religious, and political lines. As the whole human race, we separate ourselves from the Creator and the creation. We treat both with little respect and therefore suffer spiritually. Through our selfishness and shortsightedness, humanity is putting a strain on the health of our planet. We are polluting our air, water, and lands. We are aiding in the ill health and extinction of countless groups of animals and plants.

Because we appear to be materially so separate and different from each other, we easily believe in false concepts like racism and racial purity. We succumb to the feelings of differences between societies, nations, religions, and languages. We have fought, tortured, and killed each other for thousands of years over the most superficial differences among ourselves. In the last 100 years, we have had legislated racism and campaigns of racial, religious, and ideological terror throughout the world.

It is a world where we indulge every wish and seek every thrill. The stimulation of our material senses intoxicates us. We spend much of our leisure time and extra income on entertainments of all descriptions. We occupy ourselves with lavish meals, recreational drugs, adrenaline-pumping sports, and bone-jarring music. We like certain stimulations so much that we form nearly unbreakable attachments to them. Addictions of all sorts flourish.

It is a world where money itself is a business, a huge business. We have a culture of money. Many of us consider the amount of money we control as the measure of our worth and evidence of our personal status. We buy power in the economic and the political worlds. Some don't care what they can buy with it but rather use money as a way to keep score among rivals. Money is so attractive, many of us involve ourselves in an endless cycle of jobs (often jobs we don't even like) to make money to spend on ever more attractive goods and services. Many have called us "consumers," but that is just a euphemism for economic slaves. Our material lives are flourishing, but our spiritual lives are suffering.

## The Problem of Hierarchy

In our world, we have traded spiritual values for material values. We have traded spiritual identities for material identities. Through these trades, we have come to regard each other in ways that do not favor redemption. To work together to save the world, we need to make another recognition: that we are all members of the same great band of world saviors. Our materiality makes that recognition difficult. A discussion of our spiritual relationship to each other might help.

Again using the symbology of the parable of the prodigal son, we can see a great pathway from the Father's house to material existence and back. The whole of humanity is treading this great path, but we are not treading it simultaneously. Some of us have worked our way into and back out of material existence ahead of others. When we are in the Father's house, we display wholly spiritual qualities. When we are at our lowest point of materiality, we identify with matter and display material qualities. As we work our way out of materiality, we begin to lose material qualities and gain spiritual qualities. These differences—who we take ourselves to be and what degree of conscious spirituality we express—form a hierarchy. We are essentially one in spirit but are a hierarchy as we work our way through materiality at different times.

When we view it from the vantage point of spirituality, we see that this hierarchy is one of consciousness. We understand the Way (the path of return to the Father's house) to be simply a succession of states of consciousness. The Way is cyclic as is all else in nature. It is slow in the material stages and increases in speed as we move closer to the spiritual worlds. It is punctuated by dramatic breakthroughs, revelations, impressions, and insights, followed by apparently "dry periods" when we experience little if any change. For the great majority of time that we involve ourselves in the densest matter, we do not have a clue that we are even on the journey.

Those far ahead of the bulk of humanity on the path of return regard those following them as their spiritual siblings involved in the great work of redeeming the world. They can only regard them with the greatest compassion and understanding and hold them in an unshakable field of love. Those preceding us totally understand our predicament of imprisonment in materiality because it was not long ago that they too were so imprisoned. They seek only to help us and help the whole great project.

When viewed by eyes totally imprisoned by materiality, hierarchy looks dramatically different. Instead of compassion for those not as far along the path, we have a feeling of superiority or contempt or impatience. The informed and quick of mind prey on the uninformed and the slow. Monetary gains and power over others become the basis of status. Instead of a cooperative spirit, jealousy and competition reign. Material eyes see rivals and those who might be of use to personal ambition.

The less experienced are manipulated by the more experienced for strictly selfish motives. Shrewd business executives use the science of psychology to implant a desire for their product or service in those of us who are unaware of what is happening. This practice is applauded by society. People train in our schools to become proficient at this manipulation and are handsomely rewarded for their skill. This manipulation is especially practiced for products and services that no one really needs. The same process holds true in politics. Political candidates relate to the public based on the emotional "buttons" their carefully packaged personas will push, while their handlers instruct many candidates to avoid discussing or taking a firm stand on issues that are of great interest to the voters.

## Vision: Our Hope

Before we came, the world needed redemption. In our confused state of materiality, we have created a world that needs even greater redemption. The task ahead of us seems enormous. The problems facing us loom large. As one philosopher put it, these are "soul-sized" problems. And we don't seem to have "soul-sized" strength to deal with them. Instead of working together to solve our problems, the human race seems divided along racial, class, gender, economic, political, and religious lines. Instead of recognizing our diversity as a strength, each division seems pitted against the others.

Within the depths of our materiality, in the darkest part of our journey, we become aware of an urge. This urge starts quietly, but it grows in intensity as we grow more conscious of our spiritual nature. This urge is to resist the pull of the material world and to stand for what is higher, better, more true, and more beautiful. We have an urge to save the world.

This urge to save the world shows itself to us as a vision, a vision of what life would be like if everything were as it should be. Our visions are both the promise and the problem. Each of us has a vision. Some of us may think about it more, and some of us may think about it less, but we each have one. From person to person, visions might be more or less comprehensive to more or less personal.

One only has to see the look on most toddlers' faces the first time chocolate excites their taste buds. From that point on, the world simply cannot be right without chocolate. In the same way, after having a profound religious experience, the newly devoted one sees how beautiful the world would be if everyone had the same experience. A mother who lost her child to a drunken driver has a vision of a world with no drunken drivers.

We each have a unique vision, shaped by all the goodness and all the pain we have experienced. It is also shaped by our exposure to the nation, race, religion, and family into which we are born. Our vision may be crackling with compelling potency, or it may be resting in the background of our minds and hearts. We may be able to relate our vision to others easily, or it may be too vague to put into words. We may have enough facility with our inner life to be quite conscious of our vision, or we may not. But a vision is there for each of us, and it motivates our lives.

In at least two ways we can know that everyone has a vision. First, everyone has an opinion. Not everyone has an opinion about everything, but if you find the vein of a person's experience and thoughts, you will find an opinion. Our opinions arise from our visions. Opinions are how we think the world should be or should not be. The second way to know that everyone has a vision is to recognize that everyone has a conscience. Not everyone will heed that conscience, but we all have one. It is easier to heed your conscience if you have a strong conscious connection with your vision. Our conscience has its roots in our vision.

There are so many visions because the world is a big place, and there is much redeeming to do on many levels and in many specific places. Since each of us is in a unique place in the long trip back to the Father's house, each of us has a unique vision. Occasionally a human comes along with a vision that stirs our soul. Siddhartha Gautama (Buddha) gave us the vision of enlightenment in the Four Noble Truths. Jesus of Nazareth brought us a vision of divine love through the human heart. Mohandas Gandhi and Martin Luther King Jr. brought to life a vision of standing undeterred for high principles without resorting to violence. Greek philosophers had a vision of democracy, at least democracy for the privileged citizens. The founding fathers of the United States brought us the vision of the Creator endowing each one of us with the right to liberty and the freedom to choose our own path to God.

These visions strike a chord in our soul. They do not have to be argued on their merits since we instantly recognize them as Truth. Most of us realize that the Creator inspired these visions. That is another way of saying that the Creator breathed some of his Truth into the minds and hearts of these human beings, and they got to see (experience in some way) some of the Creator's vision. This experience is so compelling that these outstanding human beings have to become, live, and teach their visions. We can all be thankful that they did since they helped make all human relations more spiritual.

We tend to think that the vision we hold is our own, that we somehow created a new vision. The truth of it is that we are participating in varying degrees in one overarching vision, the Creator's vision. This vision represents the Creator's purpose for creating these multidimensional worlds. Through this vision everything exists, including us. To the part of the creation we call the human being, the Creator gave the faculty of envisioning the vision. Humans have the possibility of envisioning along with the Creator. Any human vision, no matter how small, dim, or imperfect, is but a tiny participation in the Creator's vision. For example, we say Einstein and Lincoln are men of great vision. They have in some way penetrated more fully and more clearly into the vision of the Creator, and this creates the potency of their visions.

## Vision: Our Problem

Each of us has a vision that drives us to live life the way we do. It determines what we think is right or wrong, valuable or worthless. Our vision, whether we are conscious of it or not, is sacred to us. While the sacred nature of our vision is vitalizing, it can also be a problem. Conscious contact with the Creator's vision enormously stimulates and fills us with the sense of knowing. However, we all live to some degree with the illusion of separation from the Creator and each other. That illusion distorts our view of reality. Thus, any of us can come to believe that our particular vision is the only vision, the only true vision.

Our vision is a conscious part of our connection with the Creator. The more comprehensive and inclusive the vision, the truer it is to the Creator's. The more narrow and exclusive the vision, the less true it is to the Creator's. But no matter how exclusive or inclusive the vision, it is very valuable to the holder of the vision. For most of us our vision is so valuable that we would give our lives for it.

We are hardly ever conscious that we have made contact with the vision of the Creator when it happens. We usually attribute the phenomenon to something or someone else. Prime examples of this difficulty are religious experiences. Religions are programmed instructions that, if expressly followed, will change the practitioner to be somewhat more like the Creator. After studying and practicing a religion for a time, the practitioner aligns his or her thoughts, feelings, and hopes with the Creator's vision. This synchronization allows the practitioner to experience a flash of the majesty of the Creator's vision. Yet most of us attribute the flash to the religion or to the founder of the religion instead of to the vitality of Truth.

Another example would be a dedicated scientist who has spent years studying and experimenting with the laws of nature. The scientist may not even believe in the Creator but over the years has mentally aligned his or her consciousness with the complex order, beauty, and interconnectedness of the natural world. This alignment could set up a pattern somewhat resonant with the Creator's vision and lead the scientist to an epiphany, a seeing deeper into the Creator's vision. The experience could leave the scientist convinced that diligently pursuing science had produced the experience.

Using the above examples, it would be difficult for either the scientist or the person with the religious experience to include the other's vision in his or her own vision.

The scientist had an epiphany through the study of natural laws, which did not include religion or even the idea of God. Therefore, it would be natural for the scientist to think that epiphanies arising from religious, artistic, or philosophic experiences are not based on truth. The religious practitioner, on the other hand, believes that there is only one way to such an experience and that all others are counterfeit. Both the scientist and the religious practitioner have deeply felt and tenaciously held convictions about their experiences.

Visions are powerful. Visions are glimpses of what the Creator has in mind for the creation, and they are conductors of the power of the Creator. This power can make visions living realities. Our ability to hold a vision and give it so much value is part of our participation in the great spiritualizing process. These visions are pathways through which the light of the Creator can make its way into the dark world of materiality. Visions are the mode by which perfect spiritual creations find ever more appropriate forms of expression in the unfolding material world.

What is so difficult about visions is that the individuals holding them are still partly trapped by the imperfect qualities of materiality. We exercise the power of vision in lives distorted by separation. The power impels us to bring our visions of perfection to life, yet the reality of their expression in the world is quite imperfect. We hardly ever include everyone in a vision; only the "true believers" or the "chosen ones" may take part. We see anyone outside the vision as an opponent and thus see no choice but to defend our vision in a hostile environment.

The *apparent* dissimilarity of our visions causes much of the discord in the world. Each of us believes in our own vision but not in anyone else's vision. We pit ourselves or our group against others and fight for our vision and against the vision of others.

When impelled to act, the first thing our critical minds show us is how the world is not like our vision. When we look at the world, we see wrongs and injustices. We seek to right the wrongs and punish transgressors. Here is a typical story: We become impressed by an ideal vision, and we seek to gain support by forming or joining an advocacy group. This could be a political party, a religion, or a social movement. People with similar visions join this group. The group then works for the vision and against other visions that are not similar. Together the group members try to right the wrongs and bring the vision to life. However, the vision does not include everyone, and this has two effects: it hardens the group's position and that of the opposition. Some degree of war follows—a war of words or a physical war. In war one side wins or loses.

Winning, however, is never really winning. Often, the losing side harbors ill will toward the winners and secretly seeks to undermine their efforts. Forcing the vision on the losers just makes the situation worse. Peace is an enforced, not a true peace. Usually, any advantage gained by the conflict is only for the winners, and the losers usually have to do without. Losers do not include themselves in the vision of the winners because they truly cannot see it or agree with it, although the winners may force them to give lip service to it. The holders of the losing vision start to build advocacy groups to fight the winners, and the whole process repeats itself maybe for generations. We have been following this method for millennia with continuing frustration and little redemption.

The power of our visions drives us to save the world. Our separative, material natures cause us to use this power to fight, hurt, intimidate, and kill each other in the name of goodness. In this confusion, the very process of redemption seems to work against itself. It is at the least a difficult and confusing process. It is amazing that we make any progress at all.

# 4

# *Unity*

> *We have flown the air like birds and swum the sea like fishes, but have yet to learn the simple act of walking the earth like brothers.*
> MARTIN LUTHER KING JR.

Our separation from each other and from the Creator is the basic cause of our suffering. No matter how egotistical, cold, or hateful we become on the surface, at our core we all want goodness to happen, and to happen for all. Our core is our spiritual self, the source of our existence. It causes us to think, feel, and move. It makes our hearts beat and causes us to breathe. It is the source of intelligence and is the basis of love and the root of our lives.[5]

Through the ages people have had visions of life lived from our core identity instead of from our personal, separated identities. These visions are always grand, inspiring,

---

[5] Much of this chapter is the result of reflecting on the Alice Bailey book *Esoteric Psychology, Vol. II* (New York: Lucis Publishing Company, 1970).

and synthetic. If one looks at these grand visions in a certain way, one sees a great similarity among them. Three themes are common to them all:

> **Plenty**: a world of plenty where none of us lack or have to fight for the important necessities for daily living and contributing
> **Peace**: a world at peace where we have put our differences and conflicts aside and where mutual goodwill characterizes our relationships
> **Unity**: a world where we are sure of our kinship in the great family of humanity, a world where we leave no one out. Unity means living, breathing brotherhood, an inclusive belonging to each other, where both our lives as individuals and our lives together as humanity are fully respected.

The concepts of plenty, peace, and unity are fundamental to every comprehensive vision. Whether it is communism, Christianity, monarchy, democracy, theocracy, socialism, or Islam, these three fundamentals are present. Whether we see the vision having its fruition only on Earth, only in heaven, or in both, all the grand, synthetic visions contain these three elements.

## The Problem Is the Order

As we discussed in the previous chapter, it is an understatement to say that we have had problems fulfilling these visions. At least part of the problem is the order in which we try to change our vision of plenty, peace, and unity into reality. There can be no plenty without peace, and there can be no peace without unity. Therefore, unity must be the basis of peace, and through unity and peace, plenty naturally results.

This is apparently law. We know it to be law because we have tried for millennia to reverse the process. When survival is our mode of living, we just want plenty: plenty of food, comfort, and protection. In the survival mode, peace is unheard of, and unity is not even a dream. When we live in the survival mode, the law of the jungle rules—might makes right. We take and threaten and kill and hurt to gain plenty for ourselves. Plenty eludes all but the strongest, and it will inevitably be taken from them when someone stronger comes along.

Living in this hellish state, humans have gradually come to know a higher law. If we band together (unity) and make agreements not to kill, threaten, harm, or steal from each other (peace), we will become more successful (plenty). This is the beginning of the rule of law.

Today we find ourselves in a confusing mix of partial unity (a paradox), partial peace, and partial plenty. We know ourselves to be brothers with some yet not with others. For example, we may be in a governmental unity (city or nation) with our neighbors yet regard them as our religious enemies. Or we may find people in the same religion fighting each other as political enemies.

For any system to work, all three—unity, peace and plenty—have to be present. And although we have tried to make the process work in reverse, the needed order is unity first, with peace and plenty as the natural results.

Unity is not something to be achieved. It is and always has been a fact that only needs to be realized. We have been realizing unity incrementally through the ages, first through the family, then through the clan, the tribe, and the nation. We have realized unity within religious systems, economic systems, and scientific systems. The next step in the progressive realization of the fact of unity will be a giant step. It will be the synthesis of all our present unities into one inclusive whole, the brotherhood of all humanity.

## The Power of Inclusion

To be realized, unity demands a vision that includes all humans, without exception. We cannot exclude anyone because he or she is of the wrong sex, age, race, or religion nor exclude anyone because he or she lives in the wrong place, comes from the wrong family, holds certain beliefs, or carries on certain activities (even antisocial ones). A vision of unity would include the likable and the unlikable, the strong and the weak, the rich and the poor, the wise and the ignorant. It would include those conscious of this vision and those not conscious of the vision. If we leave one person out, it is no longer unity.

This vision must include each human because each is an instrument of the Creator furthering and spiritualizing the creation. The vast breadth and depth of the capacities, interests, and activities of humanity reflect the enormity of the project to which we pledged ourselves eons ago. As is the way of the Creator, each human is unique and each makes a unique contribution to this grand project. Each of us is a child of our Creator and his creation. Some of us know that, and some of us do not. The vision includes all who know and all who do not know. Those who know will know for the ones who do not yet know.

Each of us is equal in spiritual stature to any of our brothers, yet each of us has a unique mix of talents, interests, limits, and liabilities in our earthly life. None of these earthly talents or liabilities in any way increases or diminishes our spiritual stature.

Holding every human being in this inclusive vision is the basis of love. It is love without exception or exclusion. It is love without conditions to be met or doctrine accepted. From this vision, love flows truly, consistently, and justly. Love lives easily within this sense of unity; it struggles and dies outside unity.

This love, the natural result of unity, is not to be confused with sentiment. Sentiment is liking and disliking. One brother might be displaying the spiritual qualities we like; that brother is easy to love. Another brother is living the material qualities we don't like; he is more difficult to love. Inclusive love is not dependent on whether we like or dislike the person. We may like or dislike a brother's physical nature or actions, emotional reactions, or thoughts, but we love him as our brother.

## The Individual Life and the Group Life

The reason that all of us do not already hold an inclusive vision of humanity is that most of us are deceived by the illusion that we are somehow living independently of each other. Many of us have convinced ourselves that we are totally self-made, autonomous beings. This illusion comes as part of life lived strictly as the personal self and for the personal self. It is the natural result of leaving the previous state of being: mass consciousness. Three states or patterns of consciousness span contemporary humanity: mass, self, and group consciousness.[6]

**Mass Consciousness.** When one is in mass consciousness, one's environment is in control, and one seems to be at the mercy of one's own bodily instincts and desires and the expectations and authority of others. The person in mass consciousness gains control over instinct and desire through the authority of the society instead of through self-discipline. In mass consciousness, one does not break the rules mostly because of the fear of punishment or disfavor from the authorities. Rules, laws, mores, and customs dictate behavior. In mass consciousness, one does not think for oneself because there is no clear sense of self. If the expert, authority, or clergy says something is thus and so, it *is* thus and so. Survival is all important and is guaranteed by strictly deferring to the chief, patriarch, matriarch, or shaman. Within the span of human consciousness today, mass consciousness is still to be found but is fading away. Examples are tribes and clans found today mostly in the rural parts of the least developed nations. Early human societies were apparently almost exclusively in mass consciousness.

**Self-consciousness.** Consciousness develops as a gradual progression from stage to stage. There are no clear demarcations as this list might suggest. Self-consciousness is a general stage that covers a long span and has its own

---

[6] This discussion on the range of human consciousness was influenced by many of the Alice Bailey books, especially *Esoteric Psychology, Vol. I* and *II* (New York: Lucis Publishing Company, 1970) and by Ken Wilber's book *A Theory of Everything* (Boston: Shambhala Publications, Inc., 2000).

steps and stages. Most humans are working their way through this state, and we will consider three subdivisions of self-consciousness.

*The Rebel and Orthodoxy.* The journey of self-consciousness begins when we start to think for ourselves. That causes us to question the traditions of mass consciousness and eventually revolt against them. This leads to life lived purely for the self, a life of hedonistic self-indulgence and self-aggrandizement. We learn that uncontrolled self-indulgence initially feels good but leads to great pain, and this causes us to reconsider all those societal rules we earlier rebelled against. We revisit law and order, society, and the church but this time out of the free choice of the self. Rather than being imposed as in mass consciousness, we choose law, mores, and dogma. From experience we choose the power of fundamentalism, the power of the tried and true.

*Science Rules.* As the mental nature of the self develops we begin to see the world as a conglomeration of natural laws and systems to learn about, experiment with, and master. Science becomes a way for the self to rule the environment instead of the reverse. We learn how to set goals and carry them to fulfillment. Worlds of possibilities open up and ambition and competition rule. There are winners and losers, and we must learn to be a winner. This kind of thinking establishes hierarchies of power and dominance. This is the power behind most of our present governments, economies, businesses, and societies.

*Turning Green (as in trees, not money).* Each progressive stage in the development of consciousness is an outgrowth of and a reaction to the excesses of the previous stage. This last stage in pure self-consciousness is a reaction to the excesses of the dominating hierarchies of the previous stage. It is a reaction to the "greed is good" philosophy that causes the resources of Earth to be squandered for personal gain. It is a reaction to the cold and calculating rationality of the previous stage. It levels hierarchies. It sees all points of view as being of equal value. Networking, community building, consensus, and multiculturalism replace hierarchy. Intuitive, inclusive thinking is valued over rationality. "Green" thinking encourages us to include the effect of our actions on our home, Earth. Not dogma, not science, but one's own point of view is what is important. Therefore, everything is relative to one's own point of view. Right and wrong is relative, not absolute, and therefore cannot be dogmatized.

**Group Consciousness.** The progression or unfoldment of human consciousness resembles a spiral. Looked at from one angle (from above), the traveler through the progressive states of consciousness appears to return full circle to the same state. From another angle we can see that it is a similar state but on a higher turn of the spiral. This is so with the unfoldment of group consciousness as well. It somewhat resembles the first state, mass consciousness, but with the addition of the faculties and realizations of self-consciousness.

In group consciousness we become aware that we live in a grand scheme. We know that our life is a part of a much greater life. Our hearts beat, Earth rotates, atoms vibrate, thoughts arise, and birds migrate because of the intention of a grand entity in which we all live, move, and have our being. Continents, civilizations, and species rise and fall as the life of this grand being blooms. The rhythmic ebb and flow of life are seen as the grand respirations.

The cyclic nature of life, consciousness, and loving intelligence are seen as the pulses of the great heart.

Group consciousness is not simply realizing that we are part of a group of our own kind. It is rather the realization that this great life has chosen to work through groups and that all the groups have distinct and integral parts to play in the great design.

Group consciousness doesn't just drop into our minds and hearts one day. Like everything else in time and space, it unfolds. Group consciousness can grow out of relationships. For example, the young couple at the birth of their first child can be catapulted into a limited form of group consciousness. The newcomer to the family causes an instant change in the perspective of the parents. The new parent will never again look at the world only through the eyes of the self. The new parent now sees what concerns the family, and this new perspective comes first. From the word and actions of Mother Teresa, we can see that her group perspective included the whole human race. All were her brothers and sisters, and she could only see them through the eyes of love.

Humanity's part in this great work has to do with our potential to think, imagine, create, manage, and order. One day we will be acting as the manager of the lower kingdoms in nature, the animals, plants, and minerals. We already manage the lower kingdoms on a rudimentary level. The impulse causing this management is, however, now mostly skewed by our selfishness. We refine, manage, and order the animals and plants either to eat them, get pleasure from them, or insure our security and comfort. We use the air, waters, and minerals for our personal needs and wants, with no thought to our effect on them.

We are selfish because most of us live within the state of self-consciousness. But many of us are tiring of and leaving self-consciousness and entering group consciousness. The enlivening vision of group consciousness is beginning to elevate many of us beyond our selfishness. We are not throwing our selfhood away, but we are realizing its sanctity in the One in whom we live. We are ready to renounce life lived for ourselves and make our lives holy. We mean "holy" in the sense of consciously giving our lives for the furtherance of the purposes of the whole life of which we are a part.

Many of us are suspicious of unity because of its confusion with the attempt of nations, ideologies, and religions to force their vision of unity on the whole world. The attempted world conquest by the Axis powers, the killing fields of Cambodia, Stalin's purges, and the Crusades stand as stark reminders. Unity cannot be coerced; it can only be recognized. Unity does not mean that everyone is forced into lockstep thought. It does not eliminate personal belief or perspective or set forth only one correct way to think. It does not mean that we all wear uniforms and work for the state.

Unity does mean that each of us sees that we are part of a greater whole. It means that we see our individuality as an asset in the great spiritualizing process. It means recognizing our diversity as a strength. But also, in unity we each have a sense of responsibility to our lives together, and we are inspired by the possibilities of what we can accomplish together. It is unity not imposed by humans but inspired by the love of our Creator.

To save the world, does everyone have to hold a vision of unity at once? No, it doesn't work that way. First, a few will hold the vision, but most will not. Holding the vision causes changes in one's life. When one lives life from that vision, a sense of unity, peace, and plenty radiates out to other people. These people can then see the truth of unity in a living, breathing person. That opens up possibilities in thought, feeling, and action that were earlier unknown. These new possibilities open the door to a deeper, more meaningful relationship to one's spiritual core. As the relationship deepens, the consciousness unfolds. One can sense the truth of unity in one's own right. Gradually, greater numbers of us can recognize the reality of unity. When adequate numbers of us perceive unity, the world consciousness shifts much like the falling pieces of glass in a kaleidoscope. Then everyone sees unity in a new way. Here our true work together will begin.

# 5

# The World Teacher
## and
# Religions

> *The founders of the great world religions,*
> *Gautama Buddha, Jesus, Lao-Tzu, Mohammed,*
> *all seem to have striven for a worldwide brotherhood of man;*
> *but none of them could develop institutions which would*
> *include the enemy, the unbeliever.*
> GEOFFERY GORER

Only through unity, the living realization of the brotherhood of humanity, do we have the opportunity of peace and the stability of plenty for each one of us. On this secure foundation, we build our common destiny, and that destiny is to save the world. Unity is not only our long-sought-for goal, it is the beginning of our true work together. Recognizing the brotherhood of humanity creates the possibility of recognizing the brotherhood of all beings, those in the lower and the higher kingdoms.[7] Closing the door of our selfish existence opens the door to understanding the dynamic purpose the Creator has for us, all of us together.

We are on our way to unity. We are tearing down the stone walls of class and are spanning the chasms between the races. We are bringing light to the mysteries of gender, and we are breaking down barriers to educational and informational affluence. We are learning of our relationship within larger and larger groups. We will not achieve universal, conscious realization of the fact of our unity overnight, and it will not be easy. However, help is on the way. Understanding the nature of this help requires that we look at some old concepts in a new light.

Of all human institutions, only religion and philosophy deal in any way with brotherhood. Philosophy generally does not engender the passionate support that religion does. This is caused in part by an implicit warning in the presentation of most religions: you should choose wisely because the state of your eternal existence depends on it. All religions teach brotherhood. However, most religious practitioners see and live brotherhood only among the true believers of their own religion. It is ironic that the system designed to bring us to the realization of brotherhood acts as one of the strongest barriers to its universal application. Because of misguided, religious exclusivity, many of us live in unfortunate circumstances of bitter divisions arising

---

[7] The concept of "higher kingdoms" may be unfamiliar to some readers. This chapter will provide a more complete explanation.

within our families, communities, and nations. Let's not forget that we don't just divide ourselves along religious lines, we often buttress these divisions with animosity and hate. From Ireland to Palestine, from Bosnia to the Sudan, we are killing people in the name of brotherhood, and in every nation there are firmly entrenched divisions between the practitioners of different religions.

To begin to understand universal brotherhood, we are going to need some help. The help is coming from beings who have a more developed consciousness than humans. Religions call them saints, prophets, gurus, and so on. Together they constitute a kingdom in nature that is more advanced than the human. Much of the help we will need to realize the fact of brotherhood will come (and is coming) from these beings, and therefore, our relationship with them will be more conscious, meaningful, and extensive.

First, we need to update our understanding of the nature of these beings. To do this, we need to leave behind some outmoded concepts we have of them. This will be easy for some of us and impossible for others. Some of us are all too comfortable in the current religious explanation, and others of us have never been comfortable in it. Some of us have convinced ourselves that any explanation other than the one we now hold has to be wrong. Others of us, who don't accept the current religious explanation, think the whole idea must be wrong; they throw the whole question of a higher kingdom out of the realm of possibility. I ask both the believers and the nonbelievers to try to put aside any preconceived ideas about religions and the higher kingdoms in order to give the following explanation a fair hearing.

## Waking Up Is Hard to Do

Earth needs redemption. We chose incarnation into dark, loveless matter to aid in the spiritualization of Earth. We are born unconscious of our true spiritual nature. In the midst of our long sleep in matter, we plan to awaken to our spiritual nature and change the unredeemed qualities of our bodies, our lives, our families, our societies, and the world to more spiritual qualities.

The Creator apparently has a real problem waking us up. It was probably difficult for us to adjust to materiality at first, but now we are immersed in and entranced by it—we are fast asleep to the spiritual worlds and *we like it*. To help us break the trance of materiality, the Creator started a system of contact and awakening that we call religion. The problems inherent in this awakening system are huge. For example, humans are at all steps and stages of awakening and returning to pure spirit. Each of us needs to be awakened from the step we are on so that we can take the next one. Another problem is geographical distribution; until lately, getting around the globe was a chore and took a long time. This lack of circulation meant that local areas developed their own characteristics and world-views. These world-views need to be considered when awakening the local inhabitants. We are of many races, nations, languages, and levels of knowledge.

Therefore, the one system of awakening had to have many faces and methods of presentation to satisfy the diversity of human conditions and states of development. Only in recent times have we come to know how many religions there are—scores of main divisions and thousands of sects and denominations—and these numbers keep changing. Old religious forms fade away while we add new ones continually. It would have been difficult for a citizen of the Roman Empire to imagine that someday people would not worship Jupiter. Ancient Aztecs would have had trouble imagining a religion without human sacrifices.

Awakening, even the tiniest bit, to the truth of spirit is an awesome experience. It so enlivens, uplifts, and transforms us that other experiences pale in comparison. This awakening experience is so important, so vital to us that we hold it and all the circumstances surrounding it as sacred. For most of us, these awakenings happen through religion. So it is natural that we hold our religions sacred. It is also natural to want to share the method and system we used to awaken.

We need to learn to not fall into the trap of the next natural, but erroneous, step we take. We think that if the awakening came to us by following a prescribed method, then following that method is the *only* way for anyone to awaken. Finding Truth by using our method causes us to reject the possibility that anyone could find Truth by using another method. So we have the adherents of any religion or sect believing with all their hearts that they have the one and only true way to God. They also believe that other religions are, at best, misguided and, at worst, an evil plot intending to steer us away from God and deliver us into the hands of darkness.

So the system that the Creator designed to awaken us to our spiritual brotherhood is causing us passionate division. Instead of seeing God's hand in all religions, we see it only in our own and see all the others as corrupted by various degrees of evil. We see brotherhood only within the members of our religion. From this viewpoint, brotherhood can happen only if the members of other religions drop their religions and wholeheartedly embrace ours. Since each religion is sacred to its followers, we end up sitting on our islands of doctrine, gazing at the other islands and shaking our heads with regret that everyone won't join in the one true way.

> *Truth is a river that is always splitting up into arms that reunite. Islanded between the arms the inhabitants argue for a lifetime as to which is the main river.*
> CYRIL CONNOLLY

We know the next higher kingdom in nature by many names: the kingdom of souls, the kingdom of God, the fifth kingdom, Christ and the saints, the spiritual hierarchy, and many others. Religions are the result of part of its work with humanity. Politics, education, philosophy, economics, art, and science are the result of some of its other work with humanity. Though we do not have much conscious relationship with the members of the fifth kingdom, they have been instrumental in bringing to life in our brains concepts of the spiritual life. Thanks to religions, we have at least some rudimentary outlines of the nature of God and our relationship to him.

The members of the fifth kingdom have accomplished their work in religions in large part by being born into the human family while retaining what they know as members of the fifth kingdom. The most realized being in the fifth kingdom has been the most active and influential along these lines. His work with humanity goes far back in our history. He has taken many human forms. He has been instrumental in starting most if not all our religions. We know him by many names. As stated earlier, Buddhists call him the Boddhisattva. Hindus call him Vishnu and Krishna. Muslims call him the Imam Mahdi. Jews call him the Messiah. Christians call him Jesus Christ. One of his primary duties is to be the World Teacher. He is charged with helping us realize that we are members of one spiritual family, the siblings of one God.

How can that be? How can there be one World Teacher, one central figure behind all the religions? If that is true, how can we know it? The next section proposes a perspective from which to consider these important issues.

## Truth, Meaning, and Symbols

Much of the division and misunderstanding between religions, especially concerning the World Teacher, arises from words. All words, written or spoken, are symbols. Symbols represent Truth, and Truth is not dependent on the symbol for existence, though the reverse is true. Truth is unchanged no matter what the symbol used to represent it or whether it is represented at all. Symbols can be good or poor representations of Truth. Meaning is the medium of relationship between Truth and its expression, the symbol.

Each of these three components, Truth, meaning, and symbol, have unique properties. The mismatch and inappropriate use of these three components cause much distress in our communications with each other and especially so in religion. This confusion leads to the inappropriate defense of the symbols we use to understand and believe in our religions. Discussing each of these three components might be of service.

Truth is real, constant, absolute, and eternal. It is without form and is the living source of the meaning and any symbol used to represent it. Yet Truth is elusive and challenging and is so different from our usual state of being that it is difficult for us to be with it.

> *Deep truth is imageless.*
> Percy Bysshe Shelley

> *There would be too great darkness,*
> *if truth had not visible signs.*
> Blaise Pascal

People who have some experience with Truth try to share what they have experienced, but generally, we do not gain the same experience they had by reading or hearing their accounts. For example, we may read Paul's account of being taken up into the third heaven,[8] but just reading it certainly does not take us there. From studying these accounts we at least get the idea that Truth is powerful, purifying, overwhelming, and awesome. Truth is also mysterious—not unknowable but surely difficult and challenging to know and live with. Truth cannot be figured out. It exists above and beyond the mental, emotional, or physical worlds. We can read or hear words about Truth and assume that we know it, but Truth is known by becoming it. Reading or hearing about it only opens the

---
[8] Acts 9:3–9.

door; we truly know it when we live it. Truth is not knowledge, it's alive.

The world of meaning is quite different. Meaning's structure is very similar to the structure of our lives: it is born, it grows, develops, and matures. With inattention, it can fade away. It changes as our relationship to Truth changes. Take for example the word "telephone." A person who has little experience with a telephone would ascribe quite a different meaning from his limited relationship with a telephone than would an executive in the telecommunications industry, yet each meaning is valid for the individual concerned. For either person, the meaning of the word "telephone" will grow and deepen with experience. It also grows and deepens with thought, meditation, study, and most importantly application.

So meaning is not Truth but rather the result of our relationship with Truth. It is our conscious understanding of Truth at any point in time. Therefore, meanings are not absolute; they change. If we are thinking about or meditating on a certain aspect of Truth, the meaning will grow and deepen. If we are not thinking about it, the meaning will fade and eventually disappear from our consciousness. From this relationship with Truth, we generate meaning. Meaning resides in the mental world and more precisely in the abstract mental world.

Problems arise when we confuse meaning with Truth. If we keep our relationship with Truth in a steady state, meaning does not change much or very quickly. In this condition, meaning seems to be constant, and we can delude ourselves into thinking that we have reached the pinnacle of meaning and have found Truth when in fact we are just stuck.

Confusion also arises when we believe that there is only one correct meaning for any symbol. There is no one true meaning. We can have agreements as to the meaning of common words, but these meanings change over time. The words "cool" and "gay" meant something quite different to people a century ago than they do today. The agreed meanings for many if not all words change over time, because the consciousness of the holders of the meanings (people) change.

If we choose to express the meanings stimulated by our relationship with Truth, we represent these meanings with symbols. We can make our own symbols as we go as artists do, or we can use the symbols of those who have earlier worked their way through the world of meaning and created symbols. Those representations can be words, sounds, pictures, shapes, portrayals of all kinds.

Many humans before us have wrestled with the same questions we struggle with: "Who am I? Why am I here? Is there any meaning to existence?" Much thought, meditation, and pondering through the ages has generated a world of meaning and a plethora of symbols attempting to represent Truth. As any of us who generates symbols, like artists, writers, philosophers, scientists, and so on, finds out rather quickly, most of our newly created symbols are not that good at representing Truth. An artist might go through a hundred canvases before the symbol comes close to representing the inspiration. A writer might rewrite a page over and over before he or she gets the words right. Think of the untold words spoken and written, and the drawings and music made, by all of humanity through all time. Most of the symbols we create are ordinary. Yet some symbols seem to be the result of inspired contact and relationship with Truth. Certain musical compositions, artistic renderings, poems, stories, and scriptures are beacons proclaiming human contact with Truth.

Do symbols have meaning themselves? Ultimately, no. They are only representations of someone's relation to Truth. However, the intent of the creator of the symbol was to convey meaning, and the creator encoded the meaning into the symbol. Yet without a meaning-generating interpreter of the symbol, it is a lifeless idol. The most profound scripture lies unrevealed before one who cannot derive its meaning. The symbol seems to be so much nonsense to the interpreter who has no relationship to the Truth inspiring the symbol.

*A person gets from a symbol the meaning he puts into it, and what is one man's comfort and inspiration is another's jest and scorn.*
JUSTICE ROBERT JACKSON

The interpreter of the symbol will produce meaning commensurate with his or her relationship to Truth. Since each of us has a unique relationship with Truth, there are as many variations of meaning ascribed to symbols as there are people. Symbols help bring meaning from the abstract mental levels to the brain. Our brain perceives symbols; our abstract mentality interprets (gives meaning to) them.

Of the many symbols, some are so true a representation of Truth that they serve to inspire the interpreter to generate a vivid meaning. Some symbols are not that good. We have to know the difference. Some symbols are dead to us. Some are dead because we know the truth represented so well that the symbol becomes clichéd. Others seem dead because the truth represented is so far ahead of our relationship to Truth as to be meaningless, at least for now. We have to know the difference between poor representations and symbols that represent meanings too far advanced for us or too far behind us.

## The Confusion

If we use any one of the names (symbols) of the World Teacher, confusion arises. If we use the word "Christ" to symbolize the World Teacher who inspired most of the present religions, most people think that the only teachings he inspired are the teachings of the Christian religion. That is true whether they are Christians, from other religions, or from no religion. If we use the word "Krishna" to symbolize the World Teacher, most people think that he only inspired the teachings of the Hindu religion. Most religions describe a World Teacher. Most believe that he took a human form to lead their specific group to a better relationship with God. Thus the use of any specific symbol or name causes us to designate him to one or another religious tradition.

Most problems we have in sharing with each other about the word-symbols and names that refer to the World Teacher arise in confusion about the Truth, meaning, or symbol used. The Truth of the World Teacher is unchanging, eternal, and powerful. The meaning of the word used is dependent on the relationship the interpreter has with the Truth of it. Once we realize that the symbol cannot change the Truth and that the meaning depends on the interpreter, which symbol we use becomes less important. Any of the names for the World Teacher can still mean the Truth of the World Teacher. Whether we are willing to let any of the many names of the World Teacher represent that Truth to us is strictly a choice we make. A person named John is still who he is whether he is known as "Juan" in Spain or not.

Yet to many of us involved in religions, the name is everything. Why are we so passionately attached to the symbol we use for the World Teacher? Why can we not see the World Teacher as inspiring religions other than our own? The answer to that lies in a problem that arises from the success of the religious experience.

Before we establish a relationship with Truth ourselves, none of the symbols of Truth mean much to us. One day however, everything changes. We are looking at a symbolic representation of Truth (the looking itself is a symbol of our deepening relationship to Truth) when a lightning bolt of meaning resulting from a brush with Truth itself electrifies our life. Your symbol and Truth itself connect, and you are eternally and indelibly changed. Truth has found a way to make itself known to you. The experience is profound, the meaning crisp and enlivening, and the symbol becomes holy to you. By "holy," I mean that Truth, a new meaning, and the symbol became whole or one. As a result, that symbol will forever represent to you living, complete Truth.

Confusion arises out of thinking that the now-holy symbol caused the whole experience. Apparently it did: you absorbed yourself in the symbol and the experience happened. The symbol itself, however, did not cause the experience. The years of hurting and wandering lost and alone without Truth, the ages of seeking after temporal/material values with increasing dissatisfaction, the years of having a heart aching for something other than life with ourselves at the center—all set the stage for and invoked your grand experience. Reaching up to the Truth and establishing a relationship with the Truth caused the experience.

The symbol provided a way for your brain to cooperate and take part clearly and fully. Yet the highly charged experience of connecting to Truth can cause the symbol itself to gain undue importance. If we have not had this whole, holy experience with any other symbol, we can fall easily under the illusion that our symbol is the only true and holy one.

The depth of our experience with Truth impels us to share, and we give and give again the symbol to others. Surprisingly, this giving can meet with very little success. At times hardly anyone responds to the symbol. This seeming lack of interest has to do with timing. If one of our friends is ready for his experience with Truth because of how far he has traveled on his long, arduous journey, and the symbol is presented in the right way, it works. Our friend has the experience, and we have a lifelong spiritual brother. Sometimes many are ready, sometimes no one is. Mostly the true experience is rare. We can see that by looking into our own lives. Deep insights and breakthroughs in consciousness are not everyday occurrences for most of us.

Other problems can result. We can fall into the trap of thinking that our holy symbol is our property and the property of the others who have used the holy symbol to engender the experience. The intensity of the experience with Truth and the apparent rejection of the holy symbol by others makes it seem most of the rest of the world rejects the only true, holy symbol and therefore rejects the meaning and the Truth. We can mistakenly see those who reject the holy symbol as enemies and evil ones.

We can also wrongly assume that even among the true believers, some use the symbol in the "wrong" way. Assuming each of us should have exactly the same relationship and experience with Truth fosters the illusion that each of us should get the same meaning from the holy symbol. In a vain effort to standardize meaning, those who "know" codify, doctrinize, and canonize the "proper" meaning. Groups of well-meaning people at almost the same stage of revelation find support in each other's meaning. After a while, the natural and sometimes subtle differences in meaning can cause a band of true believers to split into smaller and smaller groups. The longer a religion has been around, the more sects it spawns. Taking this to the extreme, it is possible eventually that one individual may regard himself as the only true believer.

## One Truth, Unique Meanings, and Diverse Symbols

Most of us do not and will not seriously study religions other than our own. If we do, we tend to do it out of a sense of arming ourselves for debate instead of trying to gain true insight. However, some of us have studied in an unbiased way most of the religions of our world. Most who do find that while the names and symbols used vary from religion to religion, surprisingly, the intended meanings are essentially similar. The idea of the Trinity is presented in almost every religion. The concept of good and evil receives some symbolic presentation in most religions. Most religions have common themes running through them: sacrifice, redemption, the sanctity of life, various states of spirituality and materiality, and an overarching reality from which creation proceeds. Most religions tell the same basic story: first, the worlds were not, and then they came to be under the influence of some magnificent creative motive. Most religions place humanity as a prized divine creation, who by some sort of disconnect now has a tenuous communication with its Creator. Most promise some kind of reunification, either on Earth or in an afterlife.

> *One of our problems today is that we are not well acquainted with the literature of the spirit. We're interested in the news of the day and the problems of the hour.*
> 
> JOSEPH CAMPBELL

Today, we have an important opportunity. We can come to the understanding that our cherished religious texts are only symbolic representations of the Truth that caused the birth of all religions. This understanding frees us to see the exhaustive and extensive work of the World Teacher, the work he has been involved in for all these many thousands of years. Looking through these eyes, we can see that religions are presentations of Truth made specific for and germane to certain places and times. If taken in their historical order of appearance, we can see them to be a progressive revelation of the nature and purpose of our Creator. The religions build on and complement each other, some emphasizing one aspect and some another like movements in a grand symphony. Each religion is meaningful and beautiful, but taken together, they are magnificent.

If we can fully free ourselves from our attachment to a specific symbol, yet deepen our relationship to Truth, the whole of creation begins to be symbolic of Truth. We can see meaning in the structure and function of the human body, Earth, the sun, chemistry, physics, history, politics, economics, astronomy, and on and on. This freeing lets the original symbols speak more clearly. When we read that Christ held up a glass of wine and said, "This is my blood," the extent of what he meant begins to dawn on us. The truth of Christ is bigger than what the life of a man can adequately symbolize. His blood is the blood of all life forms, including the grape. The brotherhood of Christ extends throughout all the kingdoms.

Whether we use the symbol of Christ or Vishnu or no religious symbol at all, the meaning of the World Teacher is something alive and growing in the hearts and minds of all human beings. It may be alive only as a seed, buried and unknown. It may be newly sprouted, fragile, yet full of hope and promise. It may be mature and fruitful. Since each of us has a unique relationship with the Truth that the word "Christ" only symbolizes, each of us will have a unique meaning for that Truth. We may use common symbols or different symbols for that Truth, but the Truth exists for us all.

There is one World Teacher. In loving response to the diversity within the human family, he has inspired many and varied presentations of Truth. These presentations have helped us contact Truth but have led to passionately held, erroneous divisions among the adherents of the different religions. We have the opportunity to heal these illusory and sometimes hostile separations. Here are some suggestions that might help in this healing:

- Decide what is Truth—what is meaning and what is only representational of Truth.

- Remember, the Truth that the World Teacher is trying to bring to life does not depend on anyone's representation of it, no matter how true or beautiful the symbol, no matter how inspired its creation. If the holy books from all religions suddenly vanished, Truth would still exist.

- Symbols of Truth (scriptures, icons, and so on) are not meaningful in and of themselves. They call for inspired generation of meaning. Inspiration comes through a relation or contact with Truth. Then and only then is the meaning of the symbol revealed.

- Many religions ask us to accept on faith that their scriptures are true. This acceptance does not relieve us from the responsibility of generating meaning from our study of those scriptures. Scriptures aren't just information to be gathered, they are coded symbols. Whether we believe them to be true or not, we still have to break the code. We can break the code only by learning to generate meaning. Meaning makes the scriptures come alive and shows us the Way. Even if we accept wise counsel from authorities as to the meaning of the scriptures, we must participate in that meaning. Even the counsel we accept will come to us by way of written or spoken symbols, and we still have to generate meaning to those symbols.

- The unfoldment of meaning is sequential; it does not happen at once. It expands and deepens as our relationship to Truth expands and deepens.

- Truth is revealed progressively. As soon as we are ready to have more revealed, writings, circumstances, people, and events find their way into our lives. Each of us finds other people at both more advanced and more rudimentary stages of revelation. Understanding this fact can clear up much confusion arising from the great spectrum of states of human consciousness. This wide range of consciousness is one reason that we are asked to refrain from judging each other.

- The World Teacher uses a variety of symbols to help us relate to Truth. Some of our spiritual siblings are using the same symbols, and some are using different symbols, sometimes quite different, than the symbols you use. The truth of the World Teacher cannot be contained in a symbol nor even very well represented by a symbol. Truth can be and is represented by many symbols. The more we open our hearts and minds to the scope, diversity, and grandeur of the truth of the World Teacher, the more apparent the need for many and varied symbols.

- Some of us are totally unconscious of the World Teacher. Some of us have no meaningful relationship with the truth he teaches through any of the symbols normally associated with religions. Some of us think of ourselves as nonreligious. Yet all people are dealing with the problems that arise from daily existence. All of us struggle to find the right way to live. Whether we know it or not, we are all being taught by the World Teacher. Sometimes he uses methods and symbols many of us do not take to be of a spiritual nature. The lessons we learn from our addictions, pain, and mistakes may be as valuable as those we learn from scriptures. This would be another reason to refrain from judging our brothers.

• Our spiritual brotherhood is a fact that does not depend on our religious beliefs any more than on our race, age, gender, or national origin. We do not have to be accepted into spiritual brotherhood. Our brotherhood is a reality we need only recognize.

# 6

# The Role of the Kingdoms in Nature

*The only possibility for our time
is the free association of men and women of like spirit...
not a handful but a thousand heroes, ten thousand heroes,
who will create a future image of what humankind can be.*
JOSEPH CAMPBELL

All the kingdoms in nature play their part in the great worldwide redemptive process. Take the example of the tree. Its nature is to send its roots down into the earth and its branches into the sky. It thereby positions itself to interface with the three states of the mineral kingdom: gas (the atmosphere), liquid (water), and solid (soil). It spends its life drawing from the mineral kingdom and lifting it (both physically and spiritually) into the next higher kingdom in nature. The tree transforms and redeems the mineral kingdom by changing it into itself, a higher kingdom. Compared to parts of the mineral kingdom that have not lived as a tree, these minerals have been spiritualized.

Even after the tree is long gone, the atoms exposed to its life are forever changed. God has touched these particles through his ingenious and beautiful creation, the tree. The death of the tree leaves behind organic matter instead of rock. Any gardener knows that it is much easier for the next plant to flourish in organic matter instead of rock. The original tree made it easier for the following generations of trees to do their work.

Animals spiritualize a lower kingdom in a similar manner. The vast majority of animals feed on the plant kingdom, thereby lifting a lower kingdom into a higher one. It is interesting to note that animals eat almost nothing directly from the mineral kingdom. With carnivorous animals the lifting is not between kingdoms but rather within the animal kingdom.

Lifting of one kingdom into a higher kingdom is reminiscent of the World Teacher's words:

> *And I, if I be lifted up from the earth,*
> *will draw all men unto me.*[9]

Plants and animals work that way because it is their nature. They are spiritualizing matter, but they don't know it. For now at least, they cannot be willing, conscious cooperators with the Creator. However, a plant drawing minerals up into the next higher kingdom is just as spiritual as the World Teacher drawing us up into the next higher kingdom. We are so focused on our own step in the spiritualization of matter that we have come to let it define spirituality. "Spiritual" means in the direction of spirit and away from

---

[9] John 12:32.

material. Becoming a tree is in the spiritual direction for a mineral but the material direction for a human. Of course we cannot become a tree; that direction is closed to humans. All the kingdoms can only ascend. Plants and animals cannot be conscious redeemers, but three groups can. The most evident group is humanity. We referred earlier to the next higher kingdom in nature, the fifth kingdom. A relatively unknown group bridges between these two kingdoms. It would help to explain the nature and function of the fifth kingdom and the bridging group.

## Kingdoms in Nature

To gain clarity about these two groups we need to explore the meanings of the kingdoms in nature. The distinctions between the mineral, plant, and animal kingdoms are plain to see. Most of us recognize humanity as a distinct kingdom, but not all. Some think that since humans have the same kind of body as animals, humans must be merely a species of animal. If the criterion for deciding what constitutes a kingdom in nature is simply a drastic difference in outer appearance, it is easy to see why there is confusion. Yet what determines a kingdom in nature is not its outer form but rather the dramatic difference in its consciousness.

To most of us, consciousness unfolds rather slowly. We have seen this in our own lifetimes. Each day seems much like the previous day; we do not seem to change a great deal from day to day. Yet if we think back to our consciousness at age seven, twenty-one, thirty-five, and so on, we can see an unfoldment of who we are and of what we are aware. Besides this gradual change, some of us have experienced quantum jumps in consciousness in our lifetimes. Quantum jumps are those sudden expansions of consciousness where we see into life and its meaning in a more profound way than before. These sudden expansions are usually regarded as spiritual or religious experiences.

A clear and enormous jump in consciousness distinguishes the human from the animal kingdom. All the kingdoms in nature have intelligence, yet intelligence takes a huge quantum jump in the human kingdom. Animals might make shelters for themselves (nests, burrows), but they do not have international architectural conferences where professionals discuss function, design, technique, and aesthetics. The Creator blessed humans with mind, which allows us to understand cause and effect and therefore be free to choose. Humans have free use of the mind (free will) to choose their future; animals do not. It is this quantum jump in intelligence that distinguishes the human kingdom from the other kingdoms in nature.

Humans use bodies similar to those of some animals. In much the same way as the tree leads the minerals into a higher kingdom, promising animals in a dim and far-distant past were chosen to undergo a process that would lead them out of the animal kingdom to form the human kingdom. They were given the chance to develop mind and consciousness of themselves as individuals. While the human body has stayed similar to an animal body, it has taken on characteristics that are distinct to the human kingdom. No human has trouble distinguishing an animal from a human , while most of the animals cannot see the difference.

## THE FIFTH KINGDOM

We could call the mineral the first, the plant the second, the animal the third, and the human the fourth kingdom in nature. Yet another kingdom, the fifth, generally goes unnoticed by the others. That it goes unnoticed is not strange if you think about it. Consider a man standing over an ant mound. The ants might be aware that something is hovering over their mound, yet they are unaware that a being from another kingdom in nature is watching them. They surely do not know what it means to be human. In the same way, the fifth kingdom lives on Earth with us but lives intentionally in such a way that its members do not attract much human awareness. They chose to stay away from human contact so that humanity could develop the faculty of mind on its own, without any observable help.

However, for millennia humans have been given the chance to become a part of this other kingdom. This kingdom has been presented to us under many names, and the entrances to it are many, yet not always evident. Most religions offer entrance to the kingdom of God or the kingdom of souls. It would seem from many religious presentations that we can enter only after death, yet death could mean dying to our humanness instead of merely the death of our physical bodies.

The price for entrance to this kingdom is our selfishness and self-absorption. The rules for entrance are simple to state, although difficult to fulfill: we are enjoined to love others as ourselves and to love God with all our heart. The divine aspect of love seems to be as central to the fifth kingdom as divine intelligence is to the fourth.

While all humans are learning something about love, some humans have learned and lived the fullness of love and have entered the fifth kingdom. Former humans—members of our redemptive group who are leading the way back to the Father's house—now compose the fifth kingdom. They have taken a quantum leap in consciousness to the state of being divine love.

The fifth kingdom does have some interaction with humanity. It is just that most humans do not recognize the members as beings of another kingdom. What distinguishes them from humans is their fullness of sacrifice, wisdom, compassion, and profound insight. Many members of the fifth kingdom have a choice whether to use a physical body or not. When their work demands it, their physical appearance is the same as that of other human beings since they use bodies indistinguishable from the human physical body. These beings have lived and worked among humanity all through the ages, many times going unnoticed and sometimes living in the public eye. Lao-Tzu, Buddha, Christ, Mohammed, Einstein, Jefferson, Moses, Gandhi, Plato, Byron, Lincoln, and many more members of this kingdom have started religions or brought special insights and understandings to humanity.

The fifth kingdom is organized hierarchically just as is the human kingdom. In both, the consciousnesses of some members are not as developed as those of others. Some members of the fifth kingdom make enormous impressions on humanity when they live among us, and some pass almost unnoticed. We may overlook their presence among us because we are expecting perfected, angelic beings who would fulfill our ideal of spirituality. Remember that most humans overlooked the World Teacher, the most advanced member of the fifth kingdom, when he lived in Palestine 2,000 years ago. Many members of the fifth kingdom, especially the ones most likely to have interactions with humans, are not perfected beings. They are still learning and growing and proceeding along the Way.

This kingdom does not exist far off in some heaven; it exists on Earth. It does not exist only in the future; it exists now. It is not our reward for good behavior, but rather it is a more powerful field of loving service to further God's will. This kingdom will not descend on Earth to the sound of trumpets; it only needs to be recognized by opening our hearts and minds to the possibility. The members of this kingdom are not sitting passively in quiet repose; they are actively trying to save the world. The doors are wide open to any of us who "seek...first the kingdom of God."[10]

## THE FIRST BROTHER

We know the very first one among our group to pass through the human experience and enter the fifth kingdom by many names. If your life experience has taken place in the Christian cultures, you would know him by the name Christ. If you have a background in Buddhism, you would know him as the Bodhisattva. Hindus call him Krishna, and Jews, the Messiah. Muslims refer to him as the Imam Mahdi. Only one individual stands behind all these names.

Being the first among us to enter the fifth kingdom, it is his honor and duty to be the World Teacher. The World Teacher takes on the responsibility of leading every human being through the human kingdom to the fifth

[10] Matt. 6:33.

kingdom, the kingdom of God. He teaches through example. In his life as Jesus 2,000 years ago, he lived all the steps and stages of this transition from the human kingdom to the kingdom of God. He was born, baptized, transfigured, crucified, and resurrected. He ascended. Each step represents an important part of the whole process. Going through this process liberates an enormous portion of the saving force, and the world is further saved. Christ went through the process for us so that we may know it by seeing a living example. However, he did not go through the process in place of us; each of us must go through the process ourselves.

While we know the World Teacher by many names, the name "Christ" causes much confusion both within Christianity, among the adherents of other religions, and among those who are nonreligious. Some explanation might be of service. The word "Christ" represents four connected but distinct concepts.

**An Aspect.** The first concept is that "Christ" is the word used in the Christian religion for an aspect of God. We find the concept of the Trinity in most religions. The Christian Trinity consists of the Father, the Son, and the Holy Ghost. The word "Christ" is sometimes used to represent the second aspect, the Son, the aspect of love. The Father is the will, purpose, or power aspect of God, while the Holy Ghost is the intelligence aspect. These aspects taken as a whole *are* God. Hinduism uses "Vishnu" to represent the second aspect, while "Bodhisattva" is similarly used in Buddhism. See table 6-1.

Since the creation exists in time and space, it is an unfolding process. The process started with God imbuing

*Table 6-1.*

## The Three Aspects of God
## Represented in Four Religious Traditions

|  | **Will** | **Love** | **Intelligence** |
|---|---|---|---|
| *Christianity's Trinity* | The Father | The Son | The Holy Ghost |
| *Buddhism's Trisharana* | Âdi-Bodhi | Bodhisattvas | Mânushi Buddha |
| *Hinduism's Trimûrti* | Shiva | Vishnu | Brahma |
| *Ageless Wisdom's Triad* | Atma | Buddhi | Manas |

matter with the aspect of intelligence. Now intelligence is built into matter. It knows how to follow natural laws like gravity and magnetism. Love, the second aspect, is in process of being built into matter. Sometime in the far distant future, the Creator will build the will aspect into matter.

**The Office.** The second concept associated with the word "Christ" is that of the office of the Christ. That office includes being the World Teacher and the head or leader of the fifth kingdom. At some point this brother of ours will move on to greater work, and another brother will hold the office.

**The Brother.** The third concept is that of an individual, our brother, who has sacrificed himself to, and become, a living, breathing display of the second aspect of God, the aspect of love. He is and always will be our brother, but the brother most transformed by the love of God.

**The Soul.** The fourth concept associated with the word "Christ" is the "Christ in you, the hope of Glory"[11] as Paul put it so eloquently. Something in each of us is opening like the bud of a beautiful flower. As it begins to unfold, we are called to enter the kingdom of God. Seeking, we find the way and become the Way. As we free ourselves from our desires, attachments, and the limitations of our lives as an individual, separate person, we find that we have entered this fifth kingdom. This process of relinquishment, this freeing of our spiritual nature, the soul, liberates the tremendously powerful saving force, and the world is further saved.

People started the Christian religion out of the profound effect Christ had on their lives, and being the World Teacher, he had a part in starting all religions. Although humans love to argue about scriptures, sometimes to the point of war, Christ showed no great respect for doctrine or dogma. He presented only the simplest of messages: Love your neighbor as yourself and love God with all your heart. He used no doctrine or dogma to exclude anyone. On the contrary, when humans tried to exclude someone by citing doctrine or scriptures, he consistently expanded the meaning of the teaching to include everyone. No religion,

---

[11] Col. 1:27.

including Christianity, has exclusive rights to Christ, the World Teacher. No religion or person owns the World Teacher. He is who he is for each of us, no matter what our religion or by what name we call him. If love is in your heart, that is the truth of the World Teacher.

While it seems to most of us that Christ left Earth after his brief life in Palestine 2,000 years ago, the truth is he never left. He still resides in a physical body on Earth, yet he is removed from most human interaction. He now waits for the opportunity to re-establish conscious contact with all his spiritual siblings living as humans. This re-establishment of conscious relations with us is both his and our destiny.

## THE WORLD SERVERS

The fifth kingdom and humanity, working together, will save the world. While humanity has generally been asleep to this possibility, the fifth kingdom has waited eons with great expectation for this collaboration. The missing ingredient needed is for humanity to awaken from its long sleep and begin to recognize its enormous common potential for saving the world. Today a group of workers alive and awake in the world, bridge the gulf in consciousness between the fifth and the fourth kingdoms. We call this group the World Servers. It is a somewhat new group composed of the humans who are actively transferring their identities to the fifth kingdom.

No organization is associated with this new group. Yet one can find its members in all nations, races, classes, and religious organizations. What identifies this group is a deep and abiding conviction that all of us are essentially divine and that, when given the proper chance, goodwill is our basic motivation. Members of this group come from all walks of life. No matter what their outer circumstances, they consistently seek to heal the divisions standing between individuals, races, religions, and nations. The members may or may not recognize themselves as part of this group. If that recognition is important in saving the world, they will know. If it is unimportant, they may not. However, members recognize a similarity of motive, vision, and working style among themselves.

This group of servers plays a pivotal role in saving the world. The consciousnesses of the fourth and fifth kingdoms are so different that an important communication problem exists between them. Beings—and human beings are no exception—exhibit consciousness as a range. Think of any individual's range of consciousness as an octave on a musical scale. We all can hit some high notes. We all can aspire and live somewhat unselfishly for a time. But sometimes we all can hit some low notes, by being hateful and doing damage to our environments and relationships, for example. It is difficult (but not impossible) to rise above our normal range of consciousness, yet it is equally difficult to fall too far below. Our actions symbolize our consciousness. Most of us know that, even if we stayed on our best behavior, our lives would not merit canonization as saints. But given even our worst behavior, it is also probably true that we will not strangle our mothers-in-law if we have a disagreement. Both possibilities are too far out of our range of consciousness.

The same is true for the fourth and fifth kingdoms, as the quantum leap in consciousness between the two is drastic. The higher kingdom, the fifth, can understand the fourth, but the reverse is just too difficult. Here is another highly hypothetical example. Suppose you were inspired to spiritualize the animal kingdom, to help its members become human. Suppose you were inspired enough to be born as a horse. (Of course, you can't really do that, but just imagine for a minute.) Suppose you have the physical body of a horse but the mind and heart you have now. Teaching horses about quantum physics, abstract art, and keeping a checkbook might present some problems. Your octaves are just too different. It would be really helpful to know some being who could bridge the gap and help translate between the horses' and your human octaves. It would

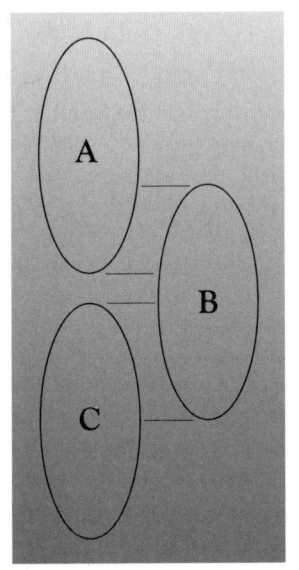

Each oval represents either a group or a person. Each occupies a range or octave of consciousness. A and C do not share any levels of consciousness, and therefore communication is difficult.

B shares some levels with both A and C and therefore acts as a bridge in consciousness between them.

B could represent the World Servers bridging the gap in consciousness between A, the fifth kingdom, and C, humanity.

▲ Increasingly spiritual levels of consciousness (the Way)

*Figure 6-1. Communication depends on overlapping levels of consciousness between groups and individuals.*

be nice to know someone who could relate somewhat to you but was just a little more "horse" than you.

This is the role that the World Servers play. Having one foot in the human kingdom and one foot in the fifth kingdom they act as translators or bridges between the two. They know love but not in its fullness. They have the sense that this is a great, divine project we are all involved in yet may not know all the particulars. They have a tremendous need to serve their fellow humans yet may not have full understanding why or even how.

World Servers work in all fields. They are advocates for advancement in whatever field they find themselves. They are innovators, but innovators with a mission. Their mission is to serve, to make life not just easier but more aligned with the truth of love. They seek a way to free their brothers and sisters from ideas, feelings, and actions that keep them prisoners of Earth. They may not be able to fulfill their mission completely, but that is precisely their value.

The method of the World Servers is to see and hold a vision of living spirituality for us all. Their work of applying the vision is frequently ineffective and flawed, but they hold the vision with the tenacity of a bull. They charge right through their failures, impelled by the strength of the vision and stimulated by their relationship (which is frequently unconscious) to the fifth kingdom. The vision finds its way into the light of day, and humanity is that much more spiritualized. Thanks to this group, concepts like the theory of relativity, democracy, forgiveness, ecology, nonviolent change, and philanthropy brighten and expand human living.

# 7

# There Is a Plan

*The absolute value of love makes life worth while,
and so makes Man's strange and difficult situation acceptable.
Love cannot save life from death;
but it can fulfill life's purpose.*
ARNOLD J. TOYNBEE

One of the most important realizations we can have is that a divine plan exists for saving the world. This plan is of such ancient origin that it precedes our understanding of human history. This plan is a design for the fulfillment of the purpose (purposes?) for which our Creator sacrificed himself. We do not call this purpose the "inscrutable will of God" for no reason. In the human condition, encumbered by our human brain consciousness, we can only experience the slightest of brushes with this purpose. To say that the Creator's purpose has to do with the redemption of the world is probably a gross reduction and distortion. In fact, redemption seems more like the method for accomplishing the purpose than the comprehensive purpose itself. When we ask why the Creator seeks to redeem the world, we open the door to an endless series of unanswerable whys: Why didn't he just create a world that didn't need redemption? So we get it redeemed, then what? Why would he need our help? We need to develop a higher faculty than the mind to gain insight into the grand purpose. Until then, redemption is the closest idea we can understand of what the Creator's purpose is.

Understanding God's purpose is difficult, but we can get some sense of the plan to fulfill the purpose. The plan reaches far into the past and far into the future. From the past, we get the sense of a great universal chaos and formlessness. So the first part of the plan had to do with bringing order out of this disorder. For purposes known only to the Creator, he chose first to imbue this great, formless chaos with his aspect of intelligence. Chaotic matter learned to be intelligent. So, where there had been only disorder, he caused ordered forms to appear. Gradations and states of matter appeared: solids, liquids, gases, and energy states. Kingdoms in nature sequentially appeared.

Not only was space (and its progeny, forms) ordered, so was time. The creation was made to display itself through cycles. The perfect creation God has "in mind" displays itself through progressive sets of forms. All forms make their appearance through a cycle of birth, growth, and death. After their death (disappearance), new forms that show greater refinement and display more spiritual qualities start their cycle. The creation displays itself through a progressive, rhythmic unfoldment of incomparable beauty, meaning, and significance.

Today we have the best display of the Creator's aspect of intelligence living and breathing on Earth—the human race. The fulfillment of the next part of the plan is to have God's second aspect, love, live and breathe on Earth. He has been preparing his vehicles, humanity and the fifth kingdom, for ages. Slowly, one at a time, humans have been prepared for the birth of love in their hearts. Divine love has been slowly germinating generally without the keen interest of humanity as a whole. Yet the blossoming of love is a process that is of supreme importance to the individuals undergoing it.

## Our Part

With that background, we come to the part we will play in the next step of the realization of the Creator's plan. He needs a field of expression, humanity, more suited than it is now to the expression of love. Our present mission is to open our hearts and minds to divine love so that it can take root in our lives and blossom on Earth.

Humanity is pivotal to the plan. *Humanity is the one kingdom in nature where spiritual states of being can exist consciously in a material body.* The kingdoms more spiritually advanced than humanity (the fifth kingdom and others) seldom exist in the material body; materiality is too unlike their nature. It would be akin to a human being trying to exist as a bacterium or a rock. The members of these advanced kingdoms are far more conscious of spiritual realities than humans are, but they cannot express them physically. The kingdoms less spiritually advanced (animals, plants, minerals) are quite material but exist totally unconscious of spirituality. These kingdoms *display* some spiritual qualities (mostly intelligence), but they fail to register spirituality consciously. Only in humanity do the two poles of existence (spirit and matter) cohabit consciously, and that is why we are of such use to the plan. There is a gap in consciousness between spirit and matter, and we are material enough and potentially spiritual enough to bridge it.

Establishing ourselves as the conscious bridge between the higher and lower kingdoms is our unique and pivotal contribution to the plan. As we become aware of the more spiritual states of being, we will naturally become aware of our role in the plan. Contact with these states of being will change us, and we will consciously improve and purify our bodies of expression (physical, emotional, and mental). Changing our bodies will also change our environments, and thereby we serve part of the plan. As we advance spiritually, we will begin to recognize our true relationship to the lower kingdoms. We will gradually drop our present exploitative relationship with them and replace it with a real interest in the development of the lower kingdoms. We will gradually come to realize that all that exists is but an expression of divinity.

Humans display and are quite conscious of the divine aspect of intelligence. Our civilizations revolve around intelligence, which shows itself through the creative use of the mind and our philosophic, artistic, scientific, and organizational talents and above all our innate adaptability. However, if we have earned our degree in intelligence, we are in kindergarten when it comes to the divine aspect of love. We do display and are somewhat conscious of love, but our material, personal natures tend to distort love in our lives. Divine love shows itself through the attributes of attraction, relation, and unity. Generally, humans tend to regard these attributes as smaller and more personal than they truly are. Our immediate contribution to the plan is understanding love in a deeper and more meaningful way and applying that understanding in our daily lives.

**Attraction.** Humans tend to think of love as attraction almost to the exclusion of the other two attributes. Most of us have found that certain substances, activities, people, or places attract us, while others repel us. We may say that we love or hate something or someone but really mean that we hold some sentiment, that we like or dislike it or him or her. We find it is pleasant or unpleasant to be with it or that person. In the extreme attraction, we have the all-consuming personal romance or even addiction. This is when we fall under the illusion that life is not worth living without the attractive person, substance, or activity. We see extreme repulsion as a lifelong unforgivable grudge, an enduring hate, or neurotic aversions to things, activities, or sensations.

We often reduce attraction to one of its most basic human expressions, sexual attraction. Emotional attraction is little evolved over sexual attraction, yet these lower expressions of love are a major interest of many interpersonal relationships. Attraction connotes poles. The interplay between the two poles—the attractor (positive pole) and the attractee (negative pole)—is magnetic. We recognize that quality in people when we say that someone has a "magnetic personality" or "charisma." Many who have charisma use it selfishly for their personal gain. Yet many others use it as it was intended: to attract others to a more meaningful or spiritual way of life.

Attraction is a part of love, but it is not all of love, and it is not confined to our personal likes and dislikes. Attraction exists in all kingdoms in nature and at all levels of consciousness. Spirit and matter attract each other, as do the fourth and fifth kingdoms. Our sun and its planets attract each other, as do electrons and protons. Men and women attract each other, as do parents and children.

**Relationship**. Like attraction, relationship is another attribute of love. Bring any two beings into awareness of each other and instead of two, we automatically have three: the two beings and their relationship. That is also true of a being and an object. When a being has awareness of an object, the being also has a relationship with it. It's true of human beings and beings on a grand scale as well. For example, the Creator caused creation, and they were automatically related. Love is the relationship of the Creator to the creation. The product of the relationship of God to the creation is the Son who is love. This relationship is cryptically stated in the Bible as "For God so loved the world, that he gave his only begotten Son."[12]

Many of us are expanding our living understanding of love by adding love's attribute of relationship to its attribute of attraction. We are beginning to understand that attraction comes and goes in our interpersonal relationships. Were we simply to follow attraction, when we stopped feeling it we would move onto the next attraction. Relationship is different, it grows and evolves. It is characterized more by a living unfoldment than it is by a sensation. Sometimes relationship burns with the sensation of attraction, and sometimes it feels cool. The truth of relationship begins to reveal itself through persistence. Love has always been there, closer than the beat of our hearts. Persistence helps us learn to stay in relationship even through the

[12] John 3:16.

inevitable dry, rocky, cold part of the journey. Persistence opens the possibility to earn a deeper understanding of love.

Relationship is the school, the research lab, and the workplace of love. Through experiment and experience, we learn what life is like both with and without love. Our cruelty, hate, and jealousy teach us as much as does the joy of unselfish caring for another. In relationship, we learn the fine distinctions between physical attraction, emotional attraction, mental attraction, and spiritual attraction. We learn that our incarnation equipment (minds, feelings, physical bodies) is flawed and impure. We learn that these impurities color and distort our view of the world and that these distortions are the root cause of all our problems and pain in relationships. From this growing understanding we learn the wisdom of taking responsibility in a relationship. We learn that it was never the other person in the relationship causing problems, it was always our own distortions. As we learn to redeem our personal defects, love flows more purely in our lives.

In relationship we learn of many other blocks to the flow of love. We learn that we can erect protective walls around ourselves that resist the flow of love and that we must develop insight and courage to destroy those walls. We see the star of selfishness lose its luster as we gain interest in the welfare of others. From within the prison of hoarding, we learn the freedom of sharing. We learn to trust the unseen spirit in a material world.

As we learn love, we learn forgiveness. In the early part of learning love, we take offense to the slings and arrows of others. We learn the lessons of shooting our arrows back and holding grudges. We learn the love-extinguishing effect of ill-will. As we grow in love, we realize that we hurt each other only in the absence of love. We begin to see a glimmer of the truth of Christ's words:

*Father, forgive them, for they know not what they do.*[13]

Our hearts go out to our brothers burdened by imperfections in their own incarnating equipment. We hold them in love even if those imperfections cause us pain. Forgiveness also connotes "giving for." Our brothers who offend us are the ones most in need of love. They, more than any, need the object of their offense (us) to stand firm in love.

We heal through relationship. As we learn to relate our spiritual and material natures, we heal, we become whole. We heal our separation from the Creator and from each other. As we heal the distortions of truth in our lives, our bodies show our healing through glowing health. As we grow in love, we can help heal the divisions within our society. It will be love living through human hearts that ends the divisions of race, economics, politics, religion, and gender.

**Unity**. The third attribute of love is unity, the realization that we are members of a greater whole. This realization is dawning on many of us today. We can use the analogy of the composition of a human being to see how we are but parts of a greater whole. A human is composed of two aspects: the bodies (physical, emotional, and mental) and the being occupying them. Together they make a complete, whole human. Physical bodies are made of organs, organs of cells, cells of molecules, molecules of atoms, and on and on. Each is both a part and a whole. An

[13] Luke 23:34.

atom is a whole atom, yet it is a part of a molecule. A cell is a whole cell and a part of an organ.

Many of us are realizing that we correspond to a cell in a much grander being. Together, human beings form an organ (some say the brain) for this being. Other kingdoms in nature form other organs. The fifth kingdom could constitute the heart. All the kingdoms together form a whole, the one in whom "we live and move and have our being."[14] Love is the energy that draws all the divergent parts into a coherent whole. This whole is attractive, magnetic, and healing. Love is the basis of relationship and communication between the parts, and between the parts and the whole. Love is the voice of the whole to the parts and of the parts to the whole.

From unity springs compassion. The meaning of compassion (Latin, *com*, "together," and *pati*, "to bear") springs from the realization that we are all bearing the weight of the unredeemed world, and we bear it together. Compassion sees no enemies. Strangers are familiar (of the family); they are simply parts of our grand family we do not yet know well. Compassion realizes the poignant difficulty of birth into materiality. Our heart goes out to all who have made that choice. From compassion springs a deep current of understanding of the predicament of our materiality, separation, confusion, and pain.

This current of understanding leads to wisdom. We enter the state of wisdom by experiencing life lived both with and without love. It involves the growing realization that the grand being of which we are a part intends that goodness and beauty live. Wisdom draws on its vast experience to fulfill that intention by intelligently applying love

[14] Acts 17:28.

in life. Wisdom realizes that applying love can happen only through sacrifice. Many of us hold the meaning of sacrifice as the "forfeiture of something highly valued." Unselfish love unlocks the original meaning (Latin, *sacer*, "sacred" plus *facere*, "to make") of making sacred or holy. In wisdom, we intentionally sacrifice our lives. In wisdom, we realize that our lives are not just our own but are part of a greater, divine life. Wisdom is love on purpose.

**Goodwill.** It is true that many of us are learning and responding to the more spiritual meanings of love. Yet how do we carry divine love into our daily lives? How do we bring love to life? Love's most important manifestation in humanity is goodwill. Through goodwill we will play our part in the Creator's plan.

Actively, consciously practiced goodwill has near magical effects. It draws us together and connects. It stimulates sharing of all kinds, including ideas, feelings, and actions. Goodwill flows from the realization that we all share a common home, predicament, responsibility, and destiny. Goodwill is compassion at work and is the "giving for" in forgiveness. It is God willing that goodness happens. It heals our personal and national animosities. Wisdom lives, practices, and teaches goodwill.

The network of our relationships is complex and extensive. We relate to the parts of ourselves, other people, our environment, institutions, other kingdoms in nature, and the whole of the greater life of which we are a part. We will play our part in the plan by making goodwill the basis of all our relationships. When this is happening in a significant part of humanity, love will have found its way to live on Earth.

## The Birth of Love

Love is finding its way. It is coming to life through the human heart, especially over the last 2,000 years. Christ's great work in Palestine two millennia ago made it possible. Christ "anchored" divine love on Earth and opened the way for love to grow. Yes, the Christian religion sprang to existence as a direct result of his life and his teachings, but love has reached much further than the Christian church and its influence. Considering the last 2,000 years, love, as goodwill, has changed our governmental, international, business, social, economic, racial, and personal relations. There has been a steadily growing trend toward philanthropy and an increasing interest in the welfare of others. We care more for the disadvantaged. We express that care through a variety of governmental, religious, and social institutions. We have made great strides in the spiritualization of human beings through education and religion.

When some people hear that, their first reaction is to say the world is *not* getting better, they see no apparent increase of love in the world. Some even see the world as "devolving" or fading away as if it were dying. The world certainly could look that way if you look only at what is wrong, if you focus on where love isn't. It is true that love isn't very strong or extensive, but that is only because of where we are in love's unfoldment. Christ's heroic anchoring of love on Earth corresponds to an act of procreation. The last 2,000 years correspond to the gestation period. Love is growing but *within* humanity. Love has still not been born, taken its first breath or its first step. Humanity generally does not love out loud yet. Love does not generally live in our constitutions, institutions, and social intercourse.

Many carry a great expectation of love, but we all know it hasn't quite happened.

The birth of love on Earth will happen like all births, when the child is ready, when it can survive on its own in the world. For love to be born, enough love has to be alive in enough hearts to recognize, nurture, and bring it to adulthood. This birth has no set date, but the child will be ready when we love enough. This is why it is important to find and express the wealth of goodwill we all hold.

Birth happens in steps and stages. We happen to be living at the end of the gestation period, the most trying time. The situation seems to be changing rapidly. Crisis seems to be lurking just behind our everyday existence. Most of us seem to be aware of an impending, drastic change. Tension is rising along with an expectancy that the drastic change will be glorious.

The birth itself has been prophesied in many scriptures for thousands of years. Portrayals of the event center around the appearance of one whom Western people would call a great savior and Eastern people an avatar. As earlier discussed, this great one is our brother, the first of our group to become divine love in its fullness. We know him by many names; use whatever name you will, but remember that others are using other names. To simplify our discussion I will use the name Christ.

Christ is the senior member of our group. Our group now spans two kingdoms in nature, the human and the fifth. The birth of love means in part that the fifth kingdom will appear to the human kingdom. Not just Christ will appear but many members of the fifth Kingdom.

The birth is near. Many people alive today will probably witness it in their lifetimes. However, they may not recognize it for what it is. Humanity has distorted the ideas and ideals surrounding Christ's reappearance among humanity. These ideas stand as more of an impediment than an aid to his return.

Many believe that he will come as a conquering king, driving out all who are full of sin and whisking his chosen few off to a peaceful place where they will be rewarded for their faithfulness. A consideration of the way Christ works will show how distorted this thinking is. Christ will never violate the free will of humanity. He wants us to choose love. He wants us to grow in love of our own accord. He wants partners in love, not robots or fearful slaves. He wants us to learn the deeper meanings of love and the value of love through our daily interaction and relationships with our brothers. He could have tried to impose love on us long ago. He could have rained fire on those who did not choose love and forced everyone through fear and intimidation. Forcing makes love a lie, and Christ knows that far better than we. Even when he is fully functioning again within humanity, he will never violate our free will. He has vision and patience.

Mostly because of the account of his reappearance in scriptures, many believe that his return will be (from the human perspective) a supernatural event. Heavenly trumpets will sound, angels will flock, and he will descend from heaven through the clouds. Considering that prophecy in the light of today's technology, we realize it is no longer supernatural to descend from the clouds. Hundreds of thousands do it every day on airplanes. And again, he has to be careful that we choose love on our own and not be unduly influenced by the supernatural. He could have seduced us with magic long ago. He surely has the power.

Yet he consistently chooses to let us learn love on our own, as he did.

Many envision a supernatural event when they read the scripture "every eye shall see him."[15] Yet that appearance would not have to be at all supernatural today. It is no coincidence that the planet is now wired for such an event. It is possible for almost every eye to see him on television or the Internet today. Will every eye recognize him? Probably not. When he came 2,000 years ago, just the tiniest group of us responded at all, and probably no one understood who he really was and how momentous was the occasion. Surely, he knew that would be the case even before he came. If he has vowed not to interfere with the free will of humanity, he surely knows today that not all, maybe not even very many of us, will recognize him at first.

Recognition might be seriously lacking for other reasons. For one, many expect his work to be confined to religion. It is true that as the World Teacher, one of his avenues of teaching will surely be religion. But who is to say that he will limit himself to that mode? He might also teach through the fields of politics, economics, education, art, or science. All are expressions of divinity through humanity. All are worthy modes of bringing light to our minds and love to our hearts.

From his perspective he takes so much more into consideration than do we when he acts. He is so much more skilled. He does not do poor or unsuccessful work. He knows what it will take to help the second aspect of God live and breathe in humanity. He knows that everything must proceed according to the laws of the Creator. He knows

---
[15] Rev. 1:7.

that all must proceed in ordered steps and stages, through ever more suitable forms of expression. As does all else, love must grow in expression through its forms in the cycles of birth, growth, and death.

It bears remembering that his return is only the birth, and maybe only the beginning of the birth, of love. What if the child grew up and became a wise, compassionate adult? What would life be like if we saw no more divisions among ourselves and realized our immense power for good? What if we lived and breathed divine, enlightened love and considered our lives as more than our own? What if we realized our lives were sacred, as billions of tiny expressions of the Creator radiating onto Earth?

There is a plan.

# 8

# *The Next Step*

> *Spirit is an invisible force made visible in all life.*
> MAYA ANGELOU

The blossoming of divine love on Earth is without doubt a spiritual event. But we must lose that distortion of our thinking that causes us to believe that spirituality shows itself only through our religions. All our efforts on Earth that seek the fulfillment of the creation are in truth spiritual. When people have a profound religious experience, they naturally think first that only their religion is sacred and the world is not. As they grow in spirituality, they realize that they must take the steps to make their whole life sacred. They take the needed steps to integrate their spiritual lives in much the same way that they earlier integrated their personal lives into a unified self. They find that they must integrate love, wisdom, goodwill, and a sense of the sacred into all aspects of their lives. Their family, social, political, business, religious, philosophical, and creative lives all become avenues for the expression of the loving spirit of God.

If this process is true in individual lives, it is also true of humanity as a whole. Divine love was engendered into the human world 2,000 years ago. Our work today is to bring a measure of love to life in all human expression. We need to bring forth a measure of spirituality into all fields of human living. In every field the outline of the next needed step is taking form.

## Work in the Economic Field

One might think that our religious infighting stands as the greatest impediment to a world ready for Christ to walk again among us. It does not. The greatest impediment lies in the field of economics as a reflection of our attitudes toward money. Expressions like "it's a dog-eat-dog world out there" aren't talking about our physical lives but rather our economic lives. Economically we are little evolved from the jungle. More than a few of us pray religiously on Sunday and then prey economically the rest of the week. This kind of activity is based on an ancient fear, the fear of scarcity, that shows itself in the way we deal with money. Sadly, many people seek wealth out of this fear.

To prepare humanity for the reappearance of Christ, the principle of sharing needs to gain a stronger hold in our personal, national, and international economic affairs. Our understanding of the principle of sharing grows from the realization that God unwaveringly shares his very life with us and provides for all our true needs. Sharing involves receiving and giving. We are conditioned by the material viewpoint to think the giving and the receiving both occur in the material world. In the principle of sharing we receive life, love, and intelligence from our Creator and share them with the world. Knowing beyond all question that God sustains us gives us freedom from the fear of scarcity. The realization of our spiritual plenty is the basis of true sharing with our brothers.

> *Infinite sharing is the law of God's inner life.*
> THOMAS MERTON

In the principle of sharing, money is not part ours and part God's. It is all God's money, and we are but his stewards. Money is just another way that God and his workers fulfill the divine plan. This may not always be the case, but for now saving the world takes money. These realizations could redirect the money that we now spend on nonessentials to the work of saving the world.

Economics is not only about money, it is about the exchange, flow, and sharing of value. Not only does an economy of money exist but also an emotional economy and an economy of ideas. We need to consider what of value we share on those levels. Have you noticed that many of us freely share our irritation and frustration with others but keep our happiness all to ourselves? Can one of us, or even a company, truly own an idea? What kind of world would it be if we freely shared our ideas instead of trying to sell them? Are they ours to sell?

Sharing does not merely mean taking money out of the hands of the rich and giving it to the poor. It means that the financially powerful begin to see their wealth as a force to help make the world more just, beautiful, capable, and ready for the World Teacher to walk again among us. It means channeling the intelligence and creativity used to generate one's money into innovative programs that make a difference in people's lives.

There are enormously creative programs today that embody these principles. An important example of such thinking is the Grameen Bank, which was started by Dr. Muhammad Yunus, a U.S.-trained economist native to Bangladesh. Instead of being an institution for giving money to poor people, this bank is a system of financial empowerment for the poorest of the poor. Small loans are made to a working group of four or five people. The pledge of the small group is the guarantee of the loan, not physical collateral. The first member of the group uses the first loan to start a business. When the loan is repaid with interest, the next member gets a loan, and so on. From the first $50 loan out of Dr. Yunus's pocket, the Grameen Bank today makes small loans that total over $30 million per month and serves people all over the globe. An estimated 10,000 borrowers are crossing the poverty line every month, and the infant mortality rate of borrowers has been cut by 34 percent. Today the Grameen Bank stands as a beacon of hope for those who have been subjected to grinding poverty for generations.[16]

Another economic illusion we need to overcome is that somehow we as individuals are living an economically independent life. Those of us who become financially successful can easily fall prey to the illusion that we are "self-made" and that if others do not have the wherewithal to make it on their own, too bad for them. In truth, each of us starts life on the shoulders of all who have passed this

---

[16] For more information about the Grameen Bank see the book by Alex Counts, *Give Us Credit* (New York: Times Books/Random House, 1996).

way before us. They have left us a wealth of experience, programs, and structure from which we can draw. Economy by its very nature is relational. If there were only one person there would be no economy. The principle of sharing really becomes meaningful when we realize that we are sharing more than money; we are in truth sharing our identity as humanity. It is not *those people* having a rough time in the Horn of Africa; *we* are having a rough time in the Horn of Africa.

For humanity to be truly helpful to the fulfillment of the plan, we need to have our basic economic requirements met without having to become economic slaves. That means not being enslaved to a job nor enslaved to the desire for material things we don't really need. Freedom from economic slavery and preoccupation with buying and selling goods will give us time to ponder the deeper meanings of life and educate ourselves. It will give us time to spend with our families and friends and the opportunity to share what is in our hearts with others. This kind of sharing is more important than we realize. It is through this sharing that we make the world ready for love.

## Work in the Political Field

To many of us, politics is in a sorry state today. It is more theater than statesmanship. It is more image than substance. Personal attack, innuendo, mudslinging, digging dirt, and demonizing are the tactics of our politics today. So little time is spent talking about the issues important to us all, we begin to wonder if we want to vote for any candidate. Those of us who are the wealthiest have always had a disproportionate influence in politics; today that disproportion is so evident as to undermine our democracy. People, including even our elected officials, have a sense of political impotence. Politics seems all too big and out of our hands, controlled by unseen forces.

These problems are the result of the politics of partisanship. Two forces oppose each other in the world, those of us who want to preserve the best of the past (the conservatives) and those of us who seek the new and innovative (the liberals). These forces are represented in all nations under various names and parties. The two forces check and goad each other to be better than what they would be alone. If we were constantly throwing out the best of the past for the untried and unproven, life would be chaos. If, however, we never admitted the new, we would choke our creativity and vivacious adaptability to death. We would become so set in our ways that our political institutions would crumble like old buildings. Each of these two opposing forces recruits adherents to its cause. The choice has traditionally been one or the other. If we join one group, we are criticized by the members of that group if we express any understanding of the other. We see it as a winner-take-all political war, and we make sure that there are winners and losers.

After years of fighting each other, many of us are tiring of and losing faith in this method. Many of us have realized that these apparently opposing forces are living within each one of us. All of us want to preserve the best of the past and be open to the promise of the future. World-sized problems need to be solved, and we won't solve them through the warfare of division, whether the war is between the rebels and the establishment or the conservatives and the liberals. Solving world-sized, soul-sized problems will take the full realization of not only who we are but also of who we are together. If we will solve these problems, we cannot afford to label and discard those of us with a different vision of the future. It will take unity. We will have to see the members of the other parties as our brothers, our spiritual brothers, our blood brothers.

> *The supreme reality of our time is*
> *our indivisibility as children of God and the*
> *common vulnerability of this planet.*
> JOHN F. KENNEDY

This vision will call for a new politics, a politics not of "either-or" but rather a politics of "both-and." With wisdom, we find that we are truly both: all of us want the best of the past to remain and the best possible future to happen. The best of the past includes the power of working with a sense of personal responsibility. The best of the future includes our potential to work with groups, up to and including the whole of humanity. We know by experience that *imposing* group consciousness on people always comes to failure, as we saw in the Soviet Union.

The realization that each one of us is both conservative and liberal opens the door to the realization that we are also something else, something very powerful. Deep within each of us is a miraculous power. It comes from the spark of the Creator that resides in each of us. It can show itself in many ways, but it comes out as our strong wish, our aim, our will that good happens. This spark is what truly drives almost all politics. This spark is, in its purest form, the impulse of the Creator willing his creation to be what he intends. The closer we align our personal wills with that divine impulse, the more true power for goodness will happen.

In a practical sense we experience this power as goodwill. We have used the word "goodwill" so often it has lost some of the power of its meaning. Yet the raw power of goodwill is awesome. It heals divisions of all descriptions: divisions between persons, between races, between religions, between nations, and even between political parties. It has the power to put us all on the same side, the side that realizes there are no sides.

If you have never experienced the power goodwill can have, try this simple experiment. Choose someone you know well. Pick a person with whom you have had a conflict or bad feelings, maybe even an argument. A political argument would be especially relevant. You could even choose a politician with whom you strongly disagree. Then, consciously place that person within your goodwill. Not all of us can do that, but if you truly can, a miracle happens. Instead of being opposed to the person, maybe even being an enemy, you become a friend. You can even begin to understand why he is as he is or why she holds those views. You probably will still not agree on every point, but the personal division between you will have lessened. You will stop placing the person in a category of disagreement and find it is only with the views that you disagree. In the purest kind of goodwill, you may even be able to see how both your view and the other view could be true. You might find that they are complementary parts of a greater whole. You might even find that we need both views to see a truer picture of reality.

We can apply this same spirit of goodwill to all our politics. We especially need it in our international politics. Unless asked, most of us would not go to our neighbors' houses and criticize their methods of conducting their households. We surely would not try to force them to change. Yet we have no problem with treating our national neighbors in such a manner. All the nations of the world need to treat each other with respect and not meddle in the internal affairs of other nations. Nations need to turn first to the needs of their own inhabitants. We need to beautify the national life; build the infrastructure; educate, house, clothe, and feed the people; care for the infirm; deal with crime; and generally work to improve the awareness and abilities of our peoples.

We do not need a world government, but we do need to realize that we are a community of nations, each having relationships with all nations. We need a forum in which we can discuss the problems that arise through our modern multifaceted interactions. We have global issues calling for a global forum where we can discuss them. The United Nations, imperfect as it is, is our best hope for such a forum. We need to improve and strengthen it instead of weaken it. It is our best hope for a world at peace.

## Work in the Field of Education

We don't need another book to tell us how bad our educational system is. We have all read how many of our students are graduating from our schools ill-prepared for the social, political, and economic worlds that await them. This is partly because of the lack of value that the former graduates, the adult public, have for our system. The public values an educational system enough to have one but not enough to be passionate advocates for it. We are generally blasé about our schools because we perceive them to be no more than a formal entrance to the world of work. And people who work in the field for which they studied in school know all too well how ill-prepared they were when they met the realities of their first job. For many of us, education was a rather boring rite of passage needed to get to our "real" lives.

Before the arrival of universal public education, we considered having a good education something of great value. We held educators in high regard, and getting an education was a much wanted and often unfulfilled dream. Why are people so passionless about education today? It seems that the answer lies in a subtle set of needs for which each person new to Earth naturally seeks fulfillment. We are passionless about our educational system because it meets these needs at best in spotty, disjointed ways.

> *The function of the university is not simply to teach bread-winning, or to furnish teachers for the public schools or to be a centre of polite society; it is, above all, to be the organ of that fine adjustment between real life and the growing knowledge of life, an adjustment which forms the secret of civilization.*
> W. E. B. Du Bois

Each of us is born innocent and totally dependent on the adults in our environment. We are also born totally uninformed about who we are, who all these other people are, what the world is, why we came here, and where we are headed. Adults are responsible for giving these newcomers an orientation that includes a way for them to find answers to these important questions. This orientation is programmed to take place over the first two to three decades of life. The first seven years primarily involves gaining facility with the physical body. The next seven years involves gaining facility with the emotional life and learning social and relational skills. The next seven years is devoted to development and control of the mind and the sense of self. Ideally, the rest of life could be centered on the development and expression of the spiritual life, the community life, and a life of service to others and God.[17]

In 1979 Dr. Robert Muller was asked to formulate a curriculum that would take into account the viewpoint he attained in decades of service at the UN, including the position of assistant secretary general. The following is a paraphrase of his response, the World Core Curriculum.

Our newcomers need to know some important facts. Newcomers need to know about their home, Earth. What is its relationship to the other heavenly bodies? What is its structure and composition? What is life? What are the kingdoms in nature? What are the building blocks of our life forms? What are the building blocks of matter?

Our newcomers need to know about the great human family into which they have been born. How many of us are here? Where do we live? How long do we live? What are our distinctions and distributions as to race, sex, age? What are our great strengths and handicaps? How do we

---

[17] I first came across many of the preceding ideas about education in the Alice Bailey book *Education in the New Age* (New York: Lucis Publishing Company, 1954).

live? What do we eat? How healthy are we? How much money do we make and spend? What work do we do? How educated are we? How do we express our spirituality and morality? They need to know about our institutions: the family; our communities, professions, corporations, and businesses; our nations, regions, and religions; our transnational organizations and networks.

Our newcomers need to know about their place in time. What is the known history, the present condition, and the possible future of our universe, our world, the human family, and our civilizations, nations, and institutions?

Our newcomers need to know about what it means to be human. How does one develop and care for the body and develop the physical senses and capacities? What are the possibilities and requirements of the various stages in our lives? They need to learn to discover and to use wisely the emotions. How does one develop one's emotional potential and wise control?

Our newcomers need to learn how to think, analyze, synthesize, conclude, and communicate. They need to learn morality and ethics as a science of logical and wholesome behavior. They need to understand the unfailing law of cause and effect and how it affects their lives and the lives of everyone else. They need to understand the relationship of their natural right to freedom with the need for a sense of responsibility. They need to know how to develop their interior or spiritual lives and establish their relationship with the Creator.[18]

The Robert Muller School, in Arlington, Texas, was the first institution to put the curriculum into action. There

[18] The World Core Curriculum is published in Dr. Robert Muller's book *New Genesis* (Golden City, NY: Doubleday & Company, Inc.).

are now over thirty schools throughout the world using this curriculum. Much of the following section on education is drawn from their work.

Our newcomers need to know that it was no accident that they were born, that they were born for a purpose, and that they can fulfill that purpose in their lifetime. While they are innocent and dependent on the adults in their environment, the adults need to relate to them in certain ways. The adults need to make the newcomers feel understood and loved. The adults need to create an atmosphere of order in both the emotional and mental environments as well as the physical environment. The adults need to teach in an atmosphere of patience, where the child is never hurried to meet adult requirements.

Teaching our newcomers is a cooperative effort among parents, schools, and religious institutions. At present, great mistrust exists among these three institutions. To present what we know to our newcomers in a seamless whole, these three institutions need to learn to connect, communicate, and trust each other. Schools and churches need to be confident that in the family the child will receive warm, personal, and loving relationships; families give children a feeling of security, a place to call home and the knowledge that someone will love them no matter what.

Parents and churches need to be confident that our schools will provide experience with the great store of human knowledge and an orientation to our life together as humanity. Parents and schools need to be confident that our religious institutions will orient our children to morality and the spiritual life.

Life works organically instead of organizationally. That means that all three institutions need to teach all three areas to our newcomers. Families, schools, and churches each need to teach loving human relationships, human knowledge, and spirituality with no restrictions imposed. Schools could teach about morality and ethics from a social and scientific point of view. Churches could teach morality and ethics from the point of view of their spiritual traditions. Families could teach morality and ethics from a loving, personal point of view. If all three points of view were complementary, and not competitive, our children would learn these truths in a more integrated fashion.

To have peace and trust about the newcomers in our charge, we would do well to rest in the assurance that each one is sent here by and watched over by the Creator of us all. The rest of us are just here to help in the best way we know.[19]

## Right Human Relations

When we take as a whole all the work to be done in the fields of economics, politics, religion, and education, we are talking about generally improving human relationships, i.e., our relationships to each other, to the other kingdoms in nature, and to our Creator. Improvement in human relations has been in process since the dawn of humanity on Earth. This process of transformation has received impulses of varying size from the Creator throughout our history. Many of these impulses have resulted in scientific and technological breakthroughs such as our understanding of fire,

---

[19] You can find more about the work of the Robert Muller School in its publication, *The World Core Curriculum: Foundations, Implementation, and Resources* (Arlington, Tex.: The Robert Muller School, 1991).

agriculture, electricity, atomic energy, and relativity. Other impulses have resulted in political and governmental breakthroughs such as the concepts of democracy and individual human rights. Many other impulses have resulted in spiritual and religious breakthroughs. However, the divine impulse 2,000 years ago, when the World Teacher lived among men, was an impulse of special importance. The scriptures symbolically portrayed the event for us as:

> *...the veil of the temple was rent in twain from the top to the bottom.*[20]

This veil is the illusion of separation from each other and from our Creator. No doubt, that great event involves more than we can yet know, but the compounding effects within humanity have been dramatic.

Important qualitative and quantitative changes have happened in the last 2,000 years. These changes started quite slowly and moved with an ever-increasing rate. The most evident change is in our sheer numbers. In the year 1000, world population was estimated to be around 340 million. By 1800, population had almost tripled to 907 million. By 1900, world population reached 1.6 billion. By 1950, we reached 2.5 billion. In 1970, we reached 3.6 billion. By the close of the twentieth century, over 6 billion people were living on Earth. In the last century we have had a fourfold increase, an increase of 4.4 billion people in the world.

The quality of our population has changed dramatically, as well. We have made amazing technological advancements.

---

[20] Mark 15:38.

At the time of the Roman Empire, most of the population was occupied with agriculture. By the late 1800s, we had harnessed the power of electricity and most humans were involved with industrial production instead of farming. Today, we are moving from industrial production to the production and communication of information. Instead of moving at the speed of an animal, a ship, or even an airplane, information now moves at the speed of light. The time it takes for events with worldwide import to register with all humans is nearly instantaneous. Satellite telecommunication and computer networks span the globe. We have been entrusted with the awesome power of atomic energy and the genetic code.

An exponential growth of interest in the welfare of others has also occurred. Scores of international relief and aid organizations have arisen mostly since the Second World War. National governments generally include at least some programs that promote the welfare of their people. Private, religious, and governmental agencies cooperate to relieve human suffering from famine, war, epidemics, and national disasters. Educational and literacy levels are improving. Basic human rights are generally afforded some protection throughout the world.

This human growth and connectivity and improvement in human welfare as outlined in the paragraphs above are evidence of the anchoring of the divine principle of love by Christ 2,000 years ago. Then, the veil of separation of humanity from God was partly torn, and the light and love of God has been stimulating the minds and hearts of humans, both individually and as a whole, ever since. This has all been happening according to the great divine plan. The next step in the plan is the reappearance of the World

Teacher and the other members of the fifth kingdom. This momentous event will herald the dawn of the fulfillment of the next stage of humanity's divine purpose on Earth.

What stands in the way of the reappearance of the World Teacher is the failure of humanity to bring to life enough goodwill for the reappearance to be useful. The World Teacher is aware of the powerful stimulation he will have on humanity when he makes himself known to the public. Divine stimulation always causes the stimulation of all qualities—both the good and the bad—in much the same way that fertilizer causes the growth of both weeds and vegetables. If he came today, certain of our expectations would cause many of us to be incredulous of his identity (the same as happened 2,000 years ago). Others would seek to claim ownership of him. His reappearance would stimulate religious, doctrinal bickering alongside political and economic turmoil. We are just not ready.

To get ready, we need to follow our hearts' simple, lovely tendency to goodwill. We need to learn to forgive. We need to forgive and put behind us all the personal, racial, religious, cultural, and national wrongs that have happened over the centuries and within our lifetimes.

People of goodwill need to come out from behind their protective walls of ideologies and doctrines so that we are cooperating together. The greatest coup of evil would be for all the people who truly want goodness to prevail to waste their opportunities by fighting and demonizing others of goodwill. Many people of goodwill are attracted to work in the religions, humanitarian causes, and political parties. It will take a special effort to see that goodwill is what is of the moment and not policy, ideology, or doctrine. If we could but realize that we are *all* trying to help the world get better, help it be more like what the Creator intended. If we could but realize that we are all in this great project *together* and that its immediate success depends on our ability to love and work with those holding different doctrines and visions. We must realize that there is but one work, the work of saving the world.

Do we have to perfect human relations before the World Teacher can reappear among us? He would be waiting a good while were that the case. We need only change the proportions of goodwill alive in the world. Enough goodwill exists today, but it is locked up in our own little worlds. It needs to be set free to reach out into the lives of others. The power of our common goodwill needs to affect the world. What we need is not just the goodwill of one religion but of all the religions, not just the goodwill of one political party but of all the parties, not the goodwill of one nation but of all nations. We need to realize that we are part of something that is much greater than our tiny lives and that our success will open the floodgates of goodness.

# 9

# Greater Things

*What's wrong with the world is, it's not finished yet.
It is not completed to that point where man can
put his final signature to the job and say,
"It is finished. We made it, and it works."*
WILLIAM FAULKNER

When Christ was near the end of his stay in the world of humanity, he made the most curious statement:

*Greater things shall ye do, because I go unto my Father.*[21]

What could be greater than making it possible for humanity to gain Christhood? What could be greater than finding his way without a predecessor or tearing the veil that separates God and his beloved humanity? What could be greater than the dramatic changes that the saving force he unleashed stimulated in humanity over the past two centuries?

Maybe the "greater things" have to do with scale. Anyone who has worked within a group on a common project

[21] John 14:12.

knows the power of a group. Something amazing comes from the variety of perspectives and abilities mixing and mingling in a group of passionate, committed people. As long as the commitment, consecration, and intention remain strong among the group members, then the bigger the group the better. The power of a group grows exponentially as the numbers increase arithmetically.

What would the scale of the release of the saving force be for a group compared to an individual? What if a group consciously walked the Way together, renounced their limitations together, and together entered the kingdom of God? The power would be incalculable. It could resound throughout the human family and help free many of us trapped by the lure of materiality and the illusion of separation. It could have a dramatic effect on the lower kingdoms in nature, speeding up their evolution and hastening the day when they might join the human kingdom and eventually the kingdom of God. When enough of the saving force has been released and Earth is more spiritualized, the change might also allow God to come even closer to Earth and "walk" among us.

We have just barely scratched the surface of the power of group. When realized, that power will make the atom's power pale by comparison. Note that the discovery of atomic power was accomplished by a small, committed group with a sense of dynamic purpose. Why are groups so disproportionately powerful? God's qualities can best show forth on Earth through suitable forms of expression. The better the form of expression, the better the demonstration. God is constantly growing and destroying forms of expression to create better ones. The same process holds true whether the form of expression is a physical body or a form of government or religion. When the life is withdrawn, the form is destroyed. For example, the feudal system of government was extremely useful at one time, but today it is all but gone. The old feudal kingdoms lost the energizing power of the divine life and have decayed and faded.

An individual human is a microcosm—a small, symbolic copy of the creating energy. The triple human nature (mind, emotions, physicality) allows the triple nature of God (will, love, intelligence or Father, Son, Holy Ghost) to resonate with some degree of similarity. Most individual humans are not that resonant (not that similar) yet, but we are working on it. And neither are our groups. Most groups are merely a convenient collection of individuals, drawn together by personal interests. A committed, consecrated group, however, with its complexity of skills and possibilities, is a better form of expression for the complexity and power of God.

We can imagine somewhat the power of a small group, but what would be the power of the whole human family, consciously working together as a grand group? How powerful it would be for humanity to do something together, all committed, all consecrated. It would shake the heavens and Earth. The power of the saving force released would be unimaginable, revealing the glory of creation. Paul spoke of that possibility when he said,

> *...the whole creation groaneth and travaileth in pain together until now...waiting for the manifestation of the Sons of God.*[22]

---

[22] Rom. 8:19–22.

The world is crying out in need, and we, the children of God, have the opportunity and the supreme responsibility to help save it. Our past prepares us while our future inspires us. All that we have been and all that we will be are forced into a single, white-hot point of convergence. It all comes together in the only place it can: *now*.

*Seize the moment. Save the world.*

# Resources

The Earth Charter—For over a decade hundreds of groups and thousands of individuals throughout the world have endeavored to create a charter that sets forth fundamental ethical principles for a sustainable way of life. Your participation is welcome. www.earthcharter.org/

Masaru Emoto—This creative and visonary Japanese researcher is the author of *The Message From Water*. This Web site shows photographs of his research with ice crystal formation. Crystals form quite different shapes under the influence of varied thoughts, feelings, and even written messages of the researchers. This is graphic evidence that what we think and feel has a profound effect on the matter in which we live. www.wellnessgoods.com/art_wat_messages.html

Global Education Associates—GEA is a partnership of individuals and organizations in 90 countries working to enable people to understand and respond constructively to the crises and opportunities of today's interdependent world. Emphasis is on the development of global ethics, values, and systems related to peace, economic well-being, ecological balance, human rights, and democratic participation. www.globaleduc.org/

Grameen Bank—Microcredit is the extension of small loans to enterpreneurs too poor to qualify for traditional bank loans. It has proven to be an effective and popular measure in the ongoing struggle against poverty. www.grameen-info.org/

Intuition in Service—This Web site helps in the awakening of the intuition and highlights its role in the creation of a better world. www.intuition-in-service.org/

Lucis Trust—The trust sponsors worldwide activities dedicated to establishing right human relations. The motivating impulse is love of God expressed through love of humanity and service of the human race.
120 Wall Street, 24th Floor
New York, NY 10005 USA
212-292-0707
newyork@lucistrust.org
www.lucistrust.org

The School of Ageless Wisdom—The school exists as a vehicle for some of those who are attracted to the study and application, respectively, of the Cosmology and Teaching of the Ageless Wisdom in a group setting.
6005 Royaloak Drive
Arlington, TX 76016 U.S.A.
rmswcc@airmail.net
www.unol.org/saw

UN University for Peace—The university is an international institution of higher education for peace created by the United Nations General Assembly in 1980.
P.O. Box 138-6100,
San José, Costa Rica
506-205-9000
info@upeace.org
www.upaz.org

Ken Wilber—*The Spectrum of Consciousness*, written when he was twenty-three years old, established him as perhaps the most comprehensive philosophical thinker of our times. He is credited with developing a unified field theory of consciousness (a synthesis and interpretation of the world's great psychological, philosophical, and spiritual traditions). His latest book is *A Theory of Everything*. wilber.shambhala.com

# Index

**A**

Acts, 9:3-9, 80
    17:28, 115-116
adults, orientation of newcomers by, 133-136
Ageless Wisdom, 6, 101
Angelou, Maya, 123
anger, 30-31
animals, 94. *See also* kingdoms in nature
aspects of God, 100-101, 108-109
atmospheres of emotions, 22-23
atoms, 26-27
attraction, 111-112
attributes of love. *See* love, attributes
autonomy, 65
avatars, 118
awakening, 76-79
awakening, religion as system of, 76
awareness, 33-34, 112

**B**

Bailey, Alice A., 6
becoming what we will redeem, 30
beings of higher kingdom, 75, 115
    *See also* fifth kingdom; kingdom of God; kingdoms in nature
birth, choosing, 22
birth of love, 117-121
brain, versus mind, 24-25
Brother aspect of Christ, 102
brotherhood, 74, 75
    of Christ, 89
    seeing, 77-78
    spiritual, 92

Buddha (Siddhartha Gautama), 54
Buddhism, 100, 101

**C**

Campbell, Joseph, 88, 93
change, 51
chaos, 27, 108
chemical qualities of Earth, 27
chitta, 25
Christ. *See also* World Teacher and Christian religion, 117
    on Earth, 103
    exclusive rights to, 103
    Office of, 101
    reappearance of, 119-121
    truth of, 89
    vision of, 54
"Christ," representations of the word, 100
Christianity, 101
Christian teachings on duality, 16
Colossians 1:27, 102
common destiny, 74-75
communication, between fourth and fifth kingdoms, 104
compassion, 115, 116
concrete mind, 35
confusion, 79-80, 81, 84-87
connection
    conscience as thread of, 19
    conscious, with Creator's vision, 55-56
    to our eternal identity, 13
Connolly, Cyril, 78
conscience, 54
conscious awareness, 33-34

conscious connection with Creator's
    vision, 55-56
consciousness
    between forth and fifth king-
        doms, 104-105
    group, 68-71, 129
    hierarchy of, 51
    mass, 66
    as a range, 104
    self-, 66-68
conscious redeemers, 95
contact and awakening, religion as
    system of, 76
convergence, 144
core of being, 37
Core Wisdom. *See* Ageless Wisdom
creation, 47, 100-101, 108
Creator, 5, 47
    our part in plan of, 109-116
    purpose of the, 107-108
    spark of the, 129-130
    vision of the, 54, 55
creators, concept of ourselves as, 47
Creator's plan, our part in, 109-116
criticism, 36, 37

**D**

"devolving" of world, 117
discrimination, 35-36, 39
divine aspect of intelligence, 110
divine impulse, 137
divine love, 109, 110, 123-124. *See
    also* love
divine plan, 107, 138-139
divine stimulation, 139
divisions of world, 48, 77-78
Doren, Mark Van, 39
duality, 13-15, 16-20
Du Bois, W. E. B., 132

**E**

Earth, qualities of matter of, 27
economic field, 124-127

education, 131-136
electromagnetic qualities of Earth, 27
Emerson, Ralph Waldo, 7
emotional atmospheres, 22-23
emotional attraction, 111
emotional body, 30
emotional states, identifying with, 10
emotional world, 22, 23, 29-34, 45
emotions, 30, 46
enlightenment, 54
entrance to kingdom of God, 97-98
eternal life, 16
evil, 139
exclusion, 64-65, 74-75
existence, 43-44

**F**

faith, acceptance of, 90-91
Father's house, 17-20, 37-38
the Father, 100
Faulkner, William, 141
fifth kingdom. *See also* kingdom of
    God; kingdoms in nature
    consciousness between forth and,
        104-105
    entrance to, 97
    heart as, 115
    hierarchy of, 98-99
    and humanity, 103
    members of, 78-79
    reappearance of members of,
        138-139
financial success, 126
First Brother, 99-103
forgiveness, 32, 113-114, 139-140
Four Noble Truths, 54
free will, 96, 119
Fromm, Erich, 19

**G**

Gandhi, Mohandas, 54
gender bias in language, 7-8
Genesis, 1:1-2, 27

God
  aspects of, 100-101, 108-109
  forms of expression for, 142-143
  kingdom of, 78-79, 97-98
  relationships with, 38
  seeking the kingdom of, 99-100
  triple nature of, 143
going home, process of, 19-20
goodwill, 104
  as attribute of love, 116
  people of, 139-140
  spirit of, 130-131
Gorer, Geoffrey, 74
Grameen Bank, 126
greater things, 141-144
Greek philosophers, 54
"green" thinking, 67-68
group consciousness, 68-71, 129
group life and individual life, 65-71
groups, power of, 141-142

## H

healing, 90-92, 114
Hegel, Georg Wilheim, 36
hierarchies, problem of, 50-52
hierarchy of fifth kingdom, 98-99
higher beings. *See* beings of higher kingdom; fifth kingdom
Hinduism, 100, 101
holy, meaning of word, 85
Holy Ghost, 100
hope, our vision for, 52-54
human, root of word, 7
humanity, 95, 98, 109
human kingdom, characteristics of, 96. *See also* kingdom of God; kingdoms in nature
human relations, 136-140
humans
  and animal kingdom, gap between, 96, 110
  aspects of, 114-115
  former, 98

human welfare, 138-139
human worlds, 37-38

## I

identity
  with emotions, 37
  existence of our, 9-10
  process of, 10-13
  separating emotions from, 32-34
  soul as higher, 39
  spiritual versus material, 50
inclusion, 64-65
inclusive vision of humanity, 65-66
individual life and group life, 65-71
inertia, 41
instincts, survival, 44
integrated self, 12
intelligence, divine aspect of, 110
interpreters, of symbols, 83
irritation, 32-34
islands of doctrine, 78

## J

Jackson, Robert, 83
Jesus. *See* Christ
John
  3:16, 112
  12:32, 94
  14:12, 141

## K

Kennedy, John F., 129
King, Martin Luther Jr., 54, 61
kingdom of God, 78-79, 99-100. *See also* fifth kingdom
kingdoms in nature. *See also* fifth kingdom
  determination of, 95-96
  higher/lower, 74, 109-110
  and humans, gap between, 96, 110
  management of lower, 68
  minerals, 93-94
  names of, 78

## L

language, gender bias in, 7-8
life
    existence of other than physical, 43-44
    main task of, 19
    orientation for skills of, 133-134
    physical relationships to matter during, 28
lifting of a kingdom, 94
limitations, our own, 15
looking at our lives, 14
losing visions, 58
love, 101. *See also* divine love
    birth of, 117-121
    divine, 109
    inclusive, 65
    qualities of, 28-29
love, attributes of
    attraction, 111-112
    goodwill, 116
    relationship, 112-114
    unity, 114-116
Luke 15:11-32, 16

## M

man, root of word, 7
manipulation, 51-52
Mark 15:38, 137
materiality, 19, 109
    imprisonment in, 51
    trance of, 43-46, 76
material worlds, 24, 45
matter
    Earth's, 27
    of the physical world, 28
    properties of, 41
    and spirit, 109-110
Matthew 6:33, 99
meaning, 79-84, 83, 91
meanings, unique, 87-92
mechanical qualities of Earth, 27
mental world, 22-25, 34-39, 45
Merton, Thomas, 125
Miller, Arthur, 10
mind, 24-25, 34-35, 46, 96
mineral kingdom, three states of, 93
money, 49-50, 125-126
Mother Teresa, 69
motivation of World Servers, 104
Muller, Robert, 133

## N

names of most realized being, 78-79
names of World Teacher, 84, 100
negative emotions, 31-33
newcomers (children), orientation of, 133-134
next step. *See* taking the next step, work of

## O

observers, 32, 37
Office of Christ, 101
One Truth, 87-92. *See also* Truth
order of changing visions, problem of, 62-63
orientation of humans for life skills, 133-134
orthodox Christian teachings on duality, 16
orthodoxy, rebel and, 67
overlapping levels of consciousness, 105

## P

parables, prodigal son, 16
parents, orientation of newcomers by, 133-136
partisanship, 128
Pascal, Blaise, 44, 80
Patanjali, 25
patterns of consciousness, 66-71
Paul
    account of the third heaven (Acts 9:3-9), 80

Col. 1:27, 102
Rom. 7:18-23, 15
Rom. 8:19-22, 143
peace, 62, 63
personalities, 47-48
personality, 46
philosophers, 54
philosophy, 74
physical body, 10, 43-44, 46, 114-115
physical redemption, 26-29
physical world, 24, 26-29, 45
plenty, 62, 63
poles of existence, 109-110
political field, 127-131
politics, 52
population of Earth, changes in, 137-138
power of groups, 141-142
problems
   of hierarchy, 50-52
   order of changing visions, 62-63
   our vision, 55-59
   of redemption, 42
   "soul-sized," 52
   world-sized, 128-129
process of identity, 10-13
procreation, Christ's anchoring of love on earth as, 117-118
prodigal son parable, 16-17, 50
projection of spiritual self, 45
properties of matter, 41
purpose for living, changes in, 12

## Q
qualities of Earth's matter, 27

## R
rational mind, 35
reappearance of Christ, 119-121, 124-125
rebel and orthodoxy, 67
recognition of physical self, 46
recognition of reappearance of Christ, 119-120
redeem, definition of, 21
redeemed versus unredeemed qualities, 37
redeemers, conscious, 95
redeeming
   in the emotional world, 29-34
   in the mental world, 34-39
   in the physical world, 26-29
   world-size problems, 42-43
redemption
   as Creator's purpose, 107-108
   of Earth, 76
   problems of, 42
relationship as attribute of love, 112-114
relationships
   with God, 38
   group consciousness and, 68
   ours, with Truth, 85
   between Truth and its expression, 79-84
religion as system of contact and awakening, 76
religions, 56
   acceptance of faith in, 90-91
   and brotherhood, 74
   entrance to kingdom of God in, 97-98
   in historical order of appearance, 88-89
   numbers of, 76-77
   unbiased study of, 87
religious exclusivity, 74-75
religious experiences, 123
religious traditions, aspects of God in, 101
repulsion, 111
Revelations 1:7, 120
revulsion to unredeemed qualities in others, 36-37
right human relations, 136-140

Robert Muller School, 134-136
Romans
   7:18-23, 15
   8:19-22, 143
rule of law, 63

### S

sacrifice, 116
saving, institutionalized, 1-2
saving force, 3-4, 19-20
saving the world, 42-43
Savior, 4, 13-15
saviors, portrayals of reappearance of, 118-119
scale of release of saving force, 141-142
science, 67
self, separation of from material, 48
selfhood, 10
self-identity, 35
selfishness, 35, 70, 113
self-oriented life, 11-12
separation of religions, 90-92
separation of self from material, 48
sexual attraction, 111
sharing, principle of, 124-126
Shelley, Percy Bysshe, 80
Siddhartha Gautama (Buddha), 54
sin, 16
slavery, 48
the Son, 100
soul, meanings of, 37-39
Soul aspect of Christ, 102
"soul-sized" problems, 52
spark of the Creator, 129-130
spirit, 77, 109-110
"spiritual," meaning of being, 94-95
spiritualization
   and transformation, 4
   of animals, 94
   of Earth, 76
   of human beings, 117
   of matter, 33, 94

spiritual levels of consciousness, 105
spiritual self, 45-46, 61
spiritual values/identities, 50
spiritual worlds, 45
structure of world of meaning, 81
survival mode, 63
symbols, 79-84
   confusion of, 81
   diverse, 87-92
   used by World Teacher, 91
synchronization with Creator's vision, 56

### T

taking bodies into three worlds, 25
taking the next step, work of
   in economic field, 124-127
   in field of education, 131-136
   in political field, 127-131
techniques for becoming an observer, 32
themes
   common religious, 88
   common to visions, 62
   saving the world, 5
The Way, 38, 51, 90-91
thinking, 10-11, 25
Thomas, Lewis, 10-11
three worlds, 24
timing, for sharing experience of Truth, 86
Toynbee, Arnold J., 107
trance of materiality, 43-46, 76
Trinity, 87-88, 100-101, 143
triple nature of humans/God, 143
Truth, 79-84
   brought by World Teacher, 90
   finding, 77
   One Truth, 87-92
   progressive revelation of, 91
   representations of, 88
   symbols of, 90
truth of Christ, 89

## U

unbiased study of religions, 87
understanding, and wisdom, 115-116
unfoldment
   of human consciousness, 68
   of meaning, 91
   of who we are, 95-96
United Nations, 131
unity, 62, 63-64
   as attribute of love, 114-116
   and common destiny, 73-74
   suspiciousness of, 70
urge to resist pull of material world, 52-53

## V

Van Doren, Mark, 39
vehicles of spiritual self, 45-46
vision
   apparent dissimilarity of, 57-58
   Creator's, 55-56
   difficulty of, 57
   including others' in our own, 56
   of life lived from core identity, 61-62
   our hope, 52-54
   our problem, 55-59
   power of, 58
   of unity, 70-71
vortex of redemption, 29-30

## W

waking up, 76-79
Way. *See* The Way
welfare of others, interest in, 138-139
winning, 58
wisdom, 6, 101, 115-116
word symbols, 79, 84-85
work. *See* taking the next step, the work of

world
   "devolving" of, 117
   divisions of, 48-49
   and ideal visions, 58
   problems of saving the, 42-43
World Core Curriculum, 133-136
World Servers, 103-106
world-sized problems, 128-129
World Teacher
   avenues of teaching of, 120
   concepts of names of, 100-101
   confusion about names of, 84
   divine impulse and, 137
   and doctrine/dogma, 102-103
   forms/names of, 79
   human consciousness of, 98-99
   presentations of Truth by, 89-90
   reappearance of, 138-139, 140
   responsibility of, 99-100
   seeing the work of, 88-89
   symbols used by, 91
   unconsciousness of, 91-92
   words of (John 12:32), 94
world we made, 47-50
"wrong" way to use symbols, 87

## Y

Yoga Sutras (Patanjali), 25
Yunus, Muhammad, 126

# SAVING THE WORLD
## Order Form

**Fax orders:** 817-429-2429. Please fill out and fax this form.
**Telephone orders:** 877-245-6813 (toll-free). In Texas call: 817-429-8299.
**Order online:** voxsophia.org
**Postal orders:** Please fill out and mail this form to Vox Sophia Publishing, 6005 Royaloak Dr., Arlington, TX 76016 USA

Name: _____

Street Address: _____

City, State, Postal Code, Country: _____

_____

E-mail: _____  Telephone: _____

**Cost of each book:** U.S. $14.95 / Canada $21.95
 (Quantity discounts available, call the publisher)
**Shipping:**
 U.S.: First book $4.00, each additional book $2.00
 International: First $9.00, additional $5.00 (est.)
**Payment method:** Check   Visa   Mastercard

Card number: _____

Name on card: _____  Exp. date: __ / __

Signature: _____